Group Processes
in Supervision

ASSOCIATION FOR SUPERVISION
AND CURRICULUM DEVELOPMENT, NEA

1201 Sixteenth Street, N.W.
Washington 6, D. C.

Copyright, 1948 by the
ASSOCIATION FOR SUPERVISION AND CURRICULUM DEVELOPMENT
NATIONAL EDUCATION ASSOCIATION
1201 Sixteenth Street, N. W.
Washington 6, D. C.

Price $1.25

Preface

The Association for Supervision and Curriculum Development is happy to add to the professional literature in the area of supervision this pamphlet, GROUP PROCESSES IN SUPERVISION. Recognition, by those responsible for programs of instruction in our schools, of the crucial task of developing skills in human relations among both the adults and children of our day has led to an increasing interest in and concern with the contributions which group planning has made and can make to improved human relations. We believe, therefore, that all Association members and all individuals interested in helping schools meet their obligations within the social structure of the present age will welcome this clear and specific statement of the role of group processes in the modern instructional program.

The pamphlet indicates clearly the primary responsibility of supervision, that of working toward improved programs of living and learning for children and youth. Its emphasis on the characteristics of a democratic school points up the importance of democratic human relations among all individuals involved in the work of the school. The analysis of the democratic group process on the basis of available research and literature in the area clearly indicates the leadership responsibility of supervisors, curriculum directors, consultants, or assistant superintendents as they work in group situations. The description of the variety of activities in which group planning has been used—and has worked—emphasizes the fact that in all efforts to improve the school the human factor is an extremely important one. In fact, the total range of the discussion is such that those who read the pamphlet should have a clearer concept of what the democratic group process is and how it can function in specific situations in order to bring about the kind of an instructional program which a modern school must have.

The Association for Supervision and Curriculum Development wishes to thank the chairman and all members of the committee of the California Association of School Supervisors who undertook the responsibility for the planning and preparation of the pamphlet, as well as all individuals who contributed in any way to the pamphlet in its final from.

Gertrude Hankamp
Executive Secretary

Committee in Charge of Preparation

LAVONE A. HANNA, Chairman
Associate Professor of Education, San
Francisco State College

WILLIAM BROWN, *Supervisor of In-Service Education, Los Angeles*

RUTH EDMANDS, *Superintendent of Schools, Colusa County*

CLARENCE FIELSTRA, *Associate Professor of Education, University of California, Los Angeles*

HOWARDINE G. HOFFMAN, *Director, Division of Elementary Education, Los Angeles County*

BERNARD LONSDALE, *Consultant in Elementary Education, California State Department of Education*

ELDA MILLS NEWTON, *Assistant Superintendent of Schools and General Supervisor, Butte County*

J. CECIL PARKER, *Associate Professor of Education, University of California, Berkeley*

DELLA M. PERRIN, *Consultant in Early Childhood Education, California State Department of Education*

DAVID RUSSELL, *Professor of Education, University of California, Berkeley*

GRETCHEN WULFING, *Supervisor of Elementary Education, Oakland*

Contents

Chapter		Page
	Introduction	7
I.	**Characteristics of a Democratic School**	9
	Lavone A. Hanna, *Associate Professor, San Francisco State College*	
II.	**Democratic Group Processes**	20
	J. Cecil Parker, *Associate Professor, University of California*	
	William P. Golden, Jr., *Instructor of English, University of San Francisco*	
III.	**Group Processes in Action**	64
	William S. Briscoe, *Assistant Superintendent, Oakland*	
	Edward C. Britton, *Director Community-School Project, Colusa County*	
	Lovelle C. Downing, *General Supervisor, Butte County*	
	Francis Drag, *Curriculum Director, San Diego County*	
	Clarence Fielstra, *Associate Professor, University of California, Los Angeles*	
	Lavone A. Hanna, *Associate Professor, San Francisco State College*	
	Don Harrison, *Assistant Superintendent, Stockton*	
	Howardine G. Hoffman, *Director of Elementary Education, Los Angeles County*	
	Youldon C. Howell, *Head Supervisor of Art Education, Pasadena*	
	Vibella Martin, *Coordinator of Curriculum, Alameda County*	
	Afton D. Nance, *Rural Supervision and Guidance, Riverside County*	
	Gladys L. Potter, *Deputy Superintendent, Long Beach*	
	Faith W. Smitter, *Coordinator Research and Guidance, Los Angeles County*	
	A. Earl Southworth, *Secondary Coordinator, San Diego County*	
	Herbert P. Stoltz, *Deputy Superintendent in Charge of Special Schools and Services, California State Department of Education*	
	Louise Wickersham, *Director Elementary Education, Burbank*	
	Helen C. Wood, *Primary Supervisor, Fresno County*	
	Gretchen Wulfing, *Supervisor Elementary Education, Oakland*	
	Bibliography	129

Introduction

This bulletin was prepared by the California Association of School Supervisors to show how group processes can be used in democratic schools by supervisors working with teachers, administrators, community leaders, and each other. The examples cited in Chapter III show that group processes can be used as successfully in large city systems as in small rural schools, with elementary as with secondary teachers, with teachers from widely scattered school districts as with those in densely populated urban communities, on curriculum projects as in community enterprises, in analyzing the needs of children as in studying the social structure of a classroom.

In Chapter I, we have attempted to point out that the chief characteristic of a democratic school is the use which it makes of group processes in stating its objectives, setting up curriculum experiences to achieve those objectives, studying the needs of children and caring for individual differences, and evaluating the success of the school's program. In Chapter II, group processes are not only defined and analyzed, but also many suggestions are made as to the "how" of putting them into operation successfully and the role which leadership must play in the process.

The supervisors who participated in the writing of this bulletin made use of group processes. The bulletin was organized by a committee which utilized all the steps of discussing, planning, deciding, acting, and evaluating. Meetings were held, ideas were shared by mail, criticism was invited, and many people participated in the final action. A conscious effort was made in planning the bulletin to get contributions from persons working in a variety of schools and at various levels, so that the reader, regardless of his supervisory position, would find a situation described which would be somewhat comparable to his own. It is our hope that other supervisors will be encouraged by this analysis of group processes and the examples of them in action to use them more widely in their schools.

Lavone A. Hanna

April 22, 1948

Characteristics of a Democratic School

All education is concerned with changing the behavior of individuals. The direction in which that change is guided and the means used to bring about the change are determined by the philosophy of the school and the society of which the school is a part. Democratic schools strive to change behavior in a direction quite different from that sought by totalitarian schools. Furthermore, they go about the process of changing behavior in different ways. Autocratic schools, whether they are in a totalitarian state or in the United States of America, are ruled by administrative fiat. In laissez-faire schools, everyone does as he pleases and the chief function of the administrator is not to interfere or upset the status quo. Democratic schools, on the other hand, make cooperative staff attacks on school problems and reach decisions as a result of group planning, discussion, action, and evaluation. Here, status factors are held at a minimum, and teachers, supervisors, administrators, and laymen work as equals on common problems. Whatever happens in the school is the concern of everyone, for what occurs in one place affects another; what appears to be an isolated problem has implications or roots in other parts of the school's program which call for concerted action.

In evaluating a school's program to ascertain whether it is a good, mediocre, or bad school; a democratic, laissez-faire, or autocratic school; a progressive, conservative, or reactionary school; one must examine the objectives, the curriculum, the environment of the school, the counseling program, the evaluation program, the morale of the faculty and student body, and the way in which policies and procedures are developed and put into operation.

A Democratic School Defines Its Objectives Clearly in Terms of the Behavioral Changes It Hopes To Bring About in Boys and Girls

The purpose or function of democratic education in the United States is the promotion of growth on the part of youth so that they become effective democratic citizens. To be effective, citizens must be well informed, physically fit, competent in work habits and in the use of the fundamental skills, critical-minded, cooperative, responsible, creative, concerned for the welfare of others, personally well adjusted, and ethical. To produce individuals who possess these characteristics is the goal of the school. But before activities can be planned or the school evaluate changes in pupil behavior, these characteristics need to be defined operationally so that teachers and pupils know what one does when he is well informed, physically fit, and the like. This is a cooperative job for teachers and pupils. The total staff should define the objectives for the school, but a teacher with her pupils needs to set up the specific behaviors expected by children at various stages of their development.

As the result of group discussions and decisions on the part of supervisors, administrators, faculty groups, and curriculum committees, one school system defined these characteristics of the effective citizen in the following way. *It is the hope of this staff that the young citizen will* increasingly *achieve these behaviors as the result of the educational experiences which it provides.*

1. *Useful information and understanding.* The effective citizen is increasingly well informed. He has a clear understanding of American traditions and ideals; has knowledge of other peoples' mode of life, their aspirations, and the problems they face; studies the question involved in establishing and maintaining a just and durable peace; understands the meaning and value of the democratic way of life and the threats which face it; understands the problems involved in earning and spending a living; understands the problem involved in living as an effective family member; knows the agencies by which public opinion is formed; studies contemporary social and economic issues, their evolution and interrelations; appreciates and understands the civil liberties; understands and uses the democratic processes; appreciates the interdependence of the peoples of the world; understands the physical and human resources of America and the peoples of the world; seeks to learn why we behave as we do; understands the influence of science on human life; recognizes the value of leisure time and the need for public recreational facilities; understands the value of personal and community health; and develops an understanding of the ethics of work.

2. *Health and physical fitness.* The effective citizen is physically fit. He shows gain in physical strength and endurance and in degree of resistance to communicable diseases; develops physical skill and muscular coordination; utilizes correct body mechanics such as sitting, walking, lifting; observes good health habits and attitudes; and engages in play activities and leisure-time pursuits.

3. *Competence in work habits and use of fundamental skills.* The effective citizen is constantly improving in his work habits and use of fundamental skills. He uses effectively such fundamental tools of learning as reading, number and space relationship; communicates his ideas clearly and concisely; uses reliable sources of information; listens courteously and with an open mind; observes skillfully; uses books and library facilities of his own volition; and is adequately prepared to carry on a trade or profession.

4. *Critical mindedness.* The effective citizen is constructively critical. He defines and analyzes problems carefully; seeks accurate and reliable information; interprets data accurately; reserves judgment until the pertinent facts have been examined; draws logical conclusions and acts in accordance with them; and recognizes the tentative nature of conclusions.

5. *Cooperation.* The effective citizen is increasingly cooperative. He is willing and able to work with others to accomplish desirable tasks; accepts the role of leader

CHARACTERISTICS OF A DEMOCRATIC SCHOOL 11

in some situations and that of follower in others; is law abiding; makes active contributions to the welfare of the group in terms of his own ability and possessions; recognizes the worth of all constructive work; sets the welfare of the group above personal interest; and works actively in the promotion of the safety and welfare of the community.

6. **Responsibility.** The effective citizen is increasingly responsible. He has in readiness the tools needed for the task; meets his obligations punctually and to the best of his ability; carries through an accepted task satisfactorily; accepts responsibility for his own growth or progress; accepts willingly the consequences of his own action or the action of his group; and respects the property and ideas of others.

7. **Creativeness.** The effective citizen is creative. He exhibits an active curiosity; finds suitable outlets for his abilities; uses leisure time wisely; seeks new and better solutions for problems; initiates improved methods of doing things; enjoys beauty and seeks to find and create the beautiful as well as the utilitarian; and utilizes many avenues through which to express his thoughts and feelings.

8. **Concern for others.** The effective citizen shows increasing social concern. He follows intelligently conventional manners and morals; realizes that his rights end when they conflict with the rights of others; governs his actions in the light of their social effect; looks upon social problems as capable of solution or amelioration; is sensitive to the problems of others and seeks to understand them; uses his abilities and talents for social good; defends the rights of minority groups; does not speak or act disparagingly of those who differ politically, religiously, economically, nationally, racially, physically, or mentally; judges an individual by his actions rather than by the social, religious, political, national, or racial group to which he belongs; acts upon the principle of the dignity and worth of each individual; and is active in aiding others when necessary without expectation of reward for so doing.

9. **Good personal adjustment.** The effective citizen is personally well adjusted and mentally healthy. He evidences freedom from undue fears, doubts, mental conflicts, feelings of inadequacy, suspicions, hatred, and envy; faces personal problems with courage and confidence; meets success and failure with poise; establishes satisfactory relationships with adults and with age-mates of both sexes; observes the accepted social customs and conventions; faces reality with confidence, and is happy and enjoys life.

10. **Ethical philosophy of life.** The effective citizen is increasingly ethical. He lives by a code embodying the best spiritual and ethical concepts; is reverent; and respects the rights of peoples to hold their beliefs and ideals.[1]

A Democratic School Provides Learning Experiences (Curriculum) Which Will Develop the Behaviors Demanded by a Democratic Society

The curriculum is the means whereby the goals of the school are achieved. It is the concern of everyone connected with the schools. In a democratic school each phase of the program is planned in relation to the total program so that there is a single coordinated program of cur-

---

[1] *Statement of Objectives of the Long Beach Public Schools* as adopted by the General Committee on the Curriculum, January 17, 1945.

riculum development on which the total staff has worked and in which everyone has an interest. Curriculum development when carried on as a group process under the leadership of skillfull supervisors and master teachers becomes an in-service project whereby teachers share experiences, challenge old and new procedures, study research findings, experiment with new techniques, and develop better practices. A democratic school thus provides learning experiences which meet the following criteria.

Relates Learning to Living

Curriculum experiences are important and authentic samples of modern living. No longer is there an over-emphasis upon the acquisition of knowledge for life in an adult world. Every effort is made to associate learning with life as it is being lived today. Language usage is not given as a memory exercise, but is learned better and remembered longer because children feel a need to express themselves clearly in writing or telling about things which are meaningful and vital to them. Arithmetic is learned in terms of things which children count, measure, and manipulate quantitatively. History, geography, and the other social studies are concerned with problems of today's world so that children and youth will understand the world in which they live and their privileges and responsibilities in that world. Excursions, such as a trip to the harbor or airport, give the pupil first-hand experience; actual objects are made a part of the classroom environment; construction and dramatics deepen understandings. The child who makes a freighter, loads it with cargo, and sends it past the lighthouse in the schoolroom harbor to a distant port has an experience which is not only meaningful but unforgettable.

Considers the Maturation of the Pupil

Satisfactory school experiences must be within the range of the pupil's interest and understanding. Until certain development takes place in the child's process of "growing up," it is wasteful and even damaging to undertake certain learnings. Consequently, consideration is given to the physical, intellectual, emotional, and social maturation of the pupil to determine readiness for specific learnings.

As yet there are few scientific studies to guide teachers and curriculum workers in the selection of experiences, although there is a growing awareness of the need for such study. Existing investigations seem to favor gradual approaches and deepening experiences rather than a specific age or grade placement which determines, once for all, when something shall be learned. The practice of teaching a child to read when he is mature enough to achieve success, rather than when he is of a legal age to enter the first grade, is an illustration of a desirable trend in applying the principle of readiness.

Utilizes the Normal Drives of Children

Growth potentialities are realized through the purposeful utilization of such natural drives as physical activity; the desire to satisfy curiosity; the urge to manipulate and construct; the impulse to participate in dramatic play and to re-enact what one sees, hears, or learns vicariously; and the inclination to share with others through oral and written expression and through expression in art, music, and rhythm. Real learning is associated with doing. From the time a baby makes his first movements, he begins to learn. As a small child he plays with his toys and seeks to know through manipulation. As he grows older new knowledge comes to him through new ways of doing, and new concepts are developed because experimentation and active participation lead him to new understandings. A passive classroom, which is devoid of worth-while activity, denies one of the first needs of childhood.

Promotes Competence in Skills for Effective Living

A program which promotes competence in skills is concerned not only with the three R's but with all basic skills necessary for effective living. Thus, the modern school is concerned not only with the skills of computation, reading, and communication, but also with skills in such fields as music, art, rhythms, dramatics, and health; with good work skills and study habits; with skills in the technique of group relationships and democratic living; and with salable skills with which the individual can become economically self-sufficient. In preparing children and youth for abundant life now and for effective living later, a good educational program gives emphasis to *all* of these skills.

Meets Children's Individual and Social Needs

In a democratic school curriculum materials are selected on the basis of the child's interests, needs, and capacities; and experiences are provided which are meaningful to him. This is the very crux of the educational program of the democratic school. Every boy and girl is entitled to the best education that society can supply. This implies not only a program adjusted to the abilities of each child so that he can progress through the schools at his own rate of maturation and development, but also a program which encourages each child to work to his maximum capacity and which releases his talents and potentialities for his own good and the betterment of society.

Provision is made for so-called normal children, exceptional children, atypical children, and all others who by their very nature need special attention to achieve maximum progress. A program which meets the needs of children will give each child opportunities to succeed, to feel wanted, to belong, and to feel secure. It will also provide experiences whereby youth will develop vocational skills, maintain physical fitness, become competent in the performance of civic responsibilities, understand the importance of family life, become wise consumers, appreciate the methods and achievements of science, develop an appreciation of the arts, develop wholesome leisure-time activities, work cooperatively with others, and grow in their ability to think rationally.[2]

Provides for the Total Development of the Child

In a world that requires fitness of all kinds, the democratic school has not fulfilled its purpose unless it provides for the development of a child's total personality. Formerly the emphasis was on only academic learnings and skills. Today the schools have failed unless they provide experiences that will give a child basic skills in academic fields; good health habits; social understandings; and opportunity to participate in activities that develop emotional stability, self-direction, good judgment, critical thinking, social poise, aesthetic appreciation, and acceptance of fine moral and spiritual concepts.

Promotes Democratic Values and Competence in Democratic Processes

In a school organized to promote the democratic way of life, experiences are provided at each grade level whereby children have opportunity for practice in the techniques of group and committee work. Each child has an opportunity to serve at times as a leader, again as a follower; to refine his ideas or efforts in light of criticism from the group; to share materials and ideas with others in order that group ends may be achieved; to have available and use materials of various kinds; to cooperate in the solution of group problems; and to find personal satisfaction in whatever makes for the welfare of the group.

Integrated units of work in both the elementary and secondary school provide opportunities for practicing democratic processes and for helping children develop a concern for the welfare of others and an appreciation of individual worth. These units help boys and girls understand the community in which they live through reconstructing and living

---

[2] National Education Association, Education Policies Commission. "Imperative Educational Needs of Youth." *Education for All American Youth*, Washington: The Commission, 1944. p. 225-26.

the life of the community or a simple primitive culture; the changes which inventions and discoveries of new ways of doing things have made in social living; how man has adjusted to, changed, or modified his environment to meet his needs; and how democratic ideals and goals may be achieved in their personal relationships and in the broad social-civic relationships of the local, state, national, and world-wide community. The study of his own and other cultures, and a study of the changes brought about by the rapid development of science and technology also help the pupil to understand that common interests have widened to encompass the entire world and that democracy is the best way which men have evolved for bringing about change by peaceful and evolutionary means.

Plans Sequential, Developmental Experiences

It is not enough that a pupil shall have many rich experiences, but the experiences must be so planned that they follow step by step the capacity of the child to acquire new concepts. They must provide an increasing challenge to his thinking and to his judgment, must stimulate his imagination in progressive stages of development, and must enlarge his understanding both in quality and in extent. To meet one of the severest criticisms of modern education, the democratic school provides a simple, inclusive plan designed so that there is continuity in the learning experience and so that the sequential experiences provide for progressively more difficult tasks and deeper and broader insight and concepts.

Provides for Flexibility and Continuous Revision

A curriculum which is sensitive to the needs of children and youth will, of necessity, reflect the society in which they live. As society changes, the content of the curriculum must change.

A good curriculum is never static. It is experimental to the extent that teachers are encouraged to be creative and resourceful, to use their initiative, and to try out new techniques and materials. The curriculum of the 1930's is no longer satisfactory for the schools of the postwar world because of the great scientific and technological advancement made during World War II. Nor can the schools return to the curriculum of a generation ago if the schools are to meet the needs of children living in an air age. Likewise, as knowledge of child growth and development increases and as new insight is gained on how learning takes place, the whole approach to learning must change. Techniques used now may be outmoded by new research just as many of those used only a few years ago have been found inefficient and unsatisfactory. Even the best curriculum must undergo constant revision in order that it may keep abreast with social change and with the evidence gathered from child study and from educational research.

Develops Experiences Cooperatively

A good curriculum is not something imposed from outside by principals, supervisors, college professors, or county or state curriculum experts. It is one developed from within by teachers with the assistance of the administrative and supervisory staff. Children, too, are consulted in planning and evaluating the learning activities. Parents contribute to the planning. Thus a good curriculum is the cooperative effort of parents, children, teachers, and administrators who are conversant with all aspects of the program and enthusiastic about it because they believe in it.[3]

A Democratic School Provides an Environment Conducive to Democratic Group Living

Although democratic education can take place in schools built for formalized, autocratic teaching, certain physical facilities make the working of group processes in the classroom easier and more successful. Movable furniture arranged for discussion in a circle or square or around tables makes it possible for the members of the class to see each other as they talk. Movable furniture can also be grouped for committee work or pushed to one side for dramatics or construction periods. New floor covering and acoustically treated walls reduce noise and make it possible for group activities to be carried on without too much confusion. Open book shelves filled with books and pamphlets invite extensive reading and research; bulletin boards, maps and globes, and access to art materials, science equipment, tools, and machinery stimulate curiosity and encourage creative activity. A well-equipped library, extensive audio-visual materials, available community resources, and the cooperation of community leaders in the utilization of the community as a laboratory for democratic learnings are all necessary parts of a school environment which is concerned in providing rich experiences for its pupils.

Group processes operate best when the group is not too large for group planning, discussion, decision, and action. Class size, therefore,

---

[3] Adapted from "The Characteristics of a Good Curriculum," developed by a group of administrators in the Long Beach Public Schools composed of Arthur W. Cox, Vivian K. Davis, Etta H. Howell, and Lavone A. Hanna.

becomes a factor in the success of group work. Certainly the pupils in classes of over twenty-five or thirty will not have as many satisfying experiences in group thinking and action as the members of smaller classes have. Taxpayers need to recognize that, if it is important for children and youth to learn to work together and become proficient in democratic group processes, the school budget must be sufficiently large to provide for a lower pupil-teacher ratio than is found in most schools.

Groupings within a class should be made to facilitate small group activity as well as to provide for certain types of instruction. Flexibility is the keynote for any grouping. Democratic living also calls for the sharing of interests and talents, for diversified and heterogeneous groups rather than the homogeneity which is sought for in some schools and by some teachers. Art teachers welcome a wide range of differences among their pupils and capitalize on these to broaden the experiences of the children, deepen their understandings, and quicken their interests.

A Democratic School Recognizes the Worth of Each Child and Provides Experiences for the Optimum Development of His Unique Talents and Personality

Not only must the curriculum be concerned with the total development of children and be designed to meet individual needs so that the talents and potentialities of all children are released and developed, but the total resources of the school must be organized for the welfare of all those who attend it. More and more, as American society has become industrialized and urbanized, and as the home has failed to perform many of its former functions, the school has had to give to many children the security, affection, success, and sense of belongingness which they need and no longer get from their families.

Good schools provide an adequate counseling program whereby guidance workers through individual and group counseling help children and young people with their personal problems so that they can make satisfactory social and educational adjustment. Here again, the democratic schools make use of the group process in attacking the personal problems of individual children. Through the case conference technique all those who are concerned with the pupil under consideration pool their knowledge, gather additional information, discuss possible courses of action, and collectively reach a decision. Involved in the process will be not only the teachers and counselors but also the doctor, the nurse, the psychiatrist (if the school has one), the principal, the supervisor, and perhaps the minister, and social worker. The school no longer is concerned with only the intellectual growth of the child. It recognizes that it may need to help a child build friendships, develop a hobby, join a club, take part in a school activity, make adjustments at home, find a place to live, get a job, or do many other things necessary for his happiness and optimum development.

A Democratic School Is One Which Constantly Evaluates Its Program and Encourages Experimentation and Change in Keeping with Social Progress and Educational Research

Corey once said that the marks of a good school were three: (a) that faculty members were dissatisfied with what they were doing; (b) that they had an idea of what would improve the situation and had the freedom to try out their ideas; and (c) that they attempted to evaluate the changes introduced.[4] Probably no school is quite so dead or frustrating as a school in which the teachers are completely satisfied with what they are doing and know all the right answers. In such a school the initiative and enthusiasm of the young teachers who join the staff are stifled within the first few months; new ideas are ridiculed as having been tried years ago and discarded; and no knowledge of new research or recent trends in education is evident in either the administration of the school or in classroom procedure. In schools where things are happening, where children are happy and eager to learn, the staff seeks to find out from each other and from supervisors and consultants new techniques and procedures which will improve their teaching. They are aided and abetted to experiment and develop new and better ways for learning by a sympathetic and helpful administration.

A Democratic School Makes Use of Group Processes in Solving Problems and Improving the Learning Situation

In democratic schools, teachers, supervisors, and administrators are conscious of group processes and continually study how they can use them more successfully. Teachers make use of sociometric and other scientific techniques in studying the social structure of their classes in order to understand the subgroups in the class and help individual pupils adjust more satisfactorily to their classmates. Pupil-teacher planning is used in setting up objectives, selecting units of work, determining how the unit will be studied, choosing committees, and evaluating progress. Likewise, supervisors and administrators recognize the importance of democratic group processes and use them in formulating policies,

---
[4] Long Beach, November 1946.

developing curriculum, selecting textbooks, planning new school buildings or remodeling old ones, putting the curriculum into operation, formulating an evaluation program, and using community resources.

Change in democratic schools may be slower than in autocratic schools. Change *by fiat* can take place much more rapidly, but it may be only a paper change. The spirit of the school and conditions in the classroom may be little modified. By working together on problems which are important to the students and faculty—discussing, planning, deciding, acting, and evaluating—the whole school will develop a new point of view and a new philosophy. The morale of teachers and students will improve because they have status in the project and an important part to play in the whole process.

Certainly the mark of a democratic school, the characteristic which best distinguishes it from other schools, is the effective use of democratic group processes at all levels: in teacher-administrator, teacher-parent, teacher-supervisor, teacher-teacher, teacher-pupil, and pupil-pupil relationships. In the hope that supervisors and curriculum directors may be helped in utilizing group processes more effectively, this bulletin is, therefore, devoted to a discussion of the characteristics and use of those processes with attention directed particularly to the role of the instructional leader.

Democratic Group Processes

Today there is an emergency in education just as vital, even if not so dramatic, as in the international scene. The need for teachers, pupils, administrators, supervisors, and parents to work together more effectively is just as critical from the long range point of view of the welfare of education and democracy as that facing the United Nations today in their efforts to work for peace. The essential skills in cooperative living can be developed only by living cooperatively. The next generation of citizens must be able to participate actively in the democratic group processes. It is imperative for the home, the school, the church, youth clubs, and civic organizations to center attention on the leadership, experiences, and methods through and in which individuals will learn to become effective group members. The outcome must be competence in effective group processes—first in relation to parents, siblings, and playmates; later in the larger demands of the community, the state, and the world. We as teachers, supervisors, and school administrators, however, cannot possibly understand the implications of living in a democratic society if we do not have daily experience in living and working in a situation where democracy operates, and if we do not acquire the skills and competencies of effective democratic group processes.

Talk-Democracy or Do-Democracy

We have been talking about the underlying concepts of democracy for years, and nearly all will agree with the talk. Unfortunately too few of us go beyond the talk stage of democracy into the doing of democracy. It is necessary, however, to restate a limited number of the assumptions upon which democratic group processes in education are based in order that we may have a point of reference on which to base our action.

- A major goal of democracy is the treatment of each individual so that he will develop to his fullest potential both as an individual and as a member of groups. In a democracy the individual is not lost in the group nor is he sacrificed to the group. The individuality of each is enhanced by cooperative action.

- The present-day community, national, and world pattern requires the knowledge and practice of techniques of cooperative group behavior as never before. It takes the best thinking and effort of many individuals and groups to solve problems today.

- One of the aims of education is to equip the individual to take his place in society— in the world of groups. The best preparation possible for this is *participation* while in school on an ever-increasing level of maturity in democratic group processes.

- The democratic way of life can be achieved most satisfactorily through a process which enhances the individual through improved working relationships with his fellow man. The process which American educators have accepted, promoted, extended, and improved is the democratic process, the outstanding characteristic of which is cooperative social action and interaction where the purposes are set by the group after inquiring into the needs of individuals who comprise it.

- The process of individual growth in cooperative, interdependent living is democracy in action. Every person in American society is a member of several groups and it is imperative that the processes through which group unification and productivity develop become a part of the experience of everyone.
- The processes of curriculum development and of improving instruction involve changing the factors interacting to shape the curriculum and the supervisory program of in-service training. Major factors are the physical environment, the desires, beliefs, knowledges, attitudes, and skills of the persons served by and serving the school. In brief, this means people changing and changing people. Changing people demands skill in the techniques of the processes of change.
- Finally, in an emerging democracy the ways of democracy need expanding so that all members of society become participants in working together. Common action is best based on group consensus in the action to be taken. Group consensus evolves from an understanding of and skill in the techniques of group action—in the techniques of Do-Democracy.

The above beliefs are not new. They have been repeated and rephrased by one educational committee after another. That is just the trouble. We are still *talking about* democracy, the democratic processes, respect for the individual, the four freedoms, and other concepts which all of us can repeat. Our need now is to recognize the ineffectiveness of mere *Talk-Democracy* and move to *Do-Democracy*. Competency in the use of democratic group processes stems from doing, from acting; it is an active process, not a passive one. Hence, if the democratic group processes are to be of value, they must be oriented in terms of a Do-Democracy as opposed to a Talk-Democracy. If we are going to stop with Talk-Democracy, there is little need to go beyond the point already reached in this bulletin for we have done the talking.

Do-Democracy: The Democratic Process

Just what is the difference between Talk-Democracy and Do-Democracy? In a very stimulating little book, *Practical Applications of Democracy*,[1] George B. de Huszar very neatly answers these questions. He describes three kinds of democracy: Talk-Democracy, Consent-Democracy, and Do-Democracy. Talk-Democracy proclaims belief in democratic ideals but does not translate belief into action; its characteristics are verbalism and inactivity. Consent-Democracy seeks to understand issues, votes "yes" or "no," protests now and then and urges that some-

---

[1] George B. de Huszar. *Practical Applications of Democracy*. New York: Harper and Brothers, 1945.

thing be done, but doesn't know what or how. It utilizes the traditional techniques of democracy which have been carefully analyzed by Bingham: the ballot, representative assembly, party politics, constitutional safeguards, federation, and fair play.[2] Consent-Democracy treats the individual as an abstraction—an isolated being representing votes. The principle problems are arithmetical—majorities and other statistics. Man-to-man relationships, the interaction of individuals and groups must go beyond the statistics to the people that make them possible.

Do-Democracy is a bending of energies by joining with other like-minded persons to get things done; its characteristics are participation with others in facing problems together and seeking intelligent solutions. Its concern is not merely how to obtain consent, but, in addition, how to create determination to participate, opportunities to participate, and skills of participation. Certainly, the right to vote once in a while does not make one an effective participant. Convincingly, de Huszar states that the question is not that of abandoning Consent-Democracy in favor of another theory of democracy, but that of supplementing and combining Consent-Democracy with Do-Democracy.

The principal methods of Do-Democracy are the democratic group processes involved in the building and using of problem-centered groups. These problem-centered groups are capable of tackling the innumerable problems of human relationships that exist in every field of activity in our society, of breaking them into simple component problems, of finding answers to these and the ultimate answers to the larger problems to which they build up. This is the principle technique of participation in Do-Democracy.

Our problem, then, is to move from Talk-Democracy to Do-Democracy. Democracy is in reality something you *do*. Action always occurs in concrete situations, in the meeting of specific problems. In many relationships and situations democracy is too much like Mark Twain's weather, "Everybody talks about it, no one does anything about it." Social structure is not something "outside and above"; it is the result of the interactions of individuals and groups. Social action, then, is primarily the multitudes of interactions in man-to-man relationships resulting in *doing*. If we are to do things democratically, it is important for us to go beyond the traditional techniques of Talk- and Consent-Democracy to Do-Democracy. Whatever is said, therefore, in this bulletin about group processes has not only *a democratic base,* but also *an action base.*

---

[2] Alfred M. Bingham. *The Techniques of Democracy.* New York: Duell, Sloan and Pearce, 1942.

Nature of Group Processes

In stating the social orientation upon which group processes are premised, no attempt was made to set any limits on the meaning of the term. Perhaps no limits can be set on the term, for inherent in the idea of process is the idea of change in ends and means. However, some attempt at describing what is meant by group processes seems imperative if the term is not going to dissipate into another piece of educational jargon. Already the term, group processes, is being used loosely; and what is worse, those who would espouse the use of group processes assume that everybody knows what is meant. Unfortunately this is not the case.

An attempt to describe group processes may well begin with the addition of the word *democratic* to the concept. When we speak of group processes, whether or not it is stated, the word *democratic* is implied. Group processes are effective in authoritarian cultures as well as in democratic ones. Under a fascist or communist society, group processes can operate effectively. In such a society the few propose and plan and do the creative thinking, and the *many* act. In a democratic society *everyone* participates creatively in the planning and delegates action to a *few* possessing special competencies as their agents. Hitler effectively misused group processes in the schools of Germany to develop race hatred, to build the idea of a superman, and to subject the individual to the state. Over a period of less than a dozen years he so directed the efforts of the schools and other educational agencies as to establish within German youth a fanatical devotion to *his* purposes. Democratic group processes must build a corresponding desire in youth to improve cooperation for democratically determined ends. Democracy does not have the copyright on group processes *per se;* one needs to differentiate sharply between the productivity of the processes as a whole and the motives which determine group action.

The Nature of a Group

Sociologists usually describe a group as the product of participating individuals and more than a sum of its constituency. Bird thinks that the distinctive characteristics of group behavior are "created by interaction."[3]

The ideas expressed by many sociologists have been synthesized by Kurt Lewin in his field theory of topological psychology. The group,

---
[3] Florian Znaniecki, "Social Groups as Products of Participating Individuals," *American Journal of Sociology*, XLIV, (May 1939). p. 799; Charles Bird, *Social Psychology*. New York: D. Appleton-Century Company, 1940. p. 808; Eduard C. Lindeman, *Social Discovery*. New York: Republic Publishing Company, 1942. p. 112.

according to Lewin, is not a superindividual entity, nor is it identical to the sum of its parts. Rather, it is a dynamic whole which has properties which are different from the properties of the parts. Like any other dynamic whole it can be defined operationally by the interdependence of its parts.[4] The basic criteria for the existence of any group of participating individuals are (a) interdependence in behavior among the members, and (b) identification of the members with the group. Interdependence among the members is basic to the group concept, for without it the psychological concept of the group is superfluous. The distinguishing criterion is the identification of the members with the group. Operationally identification is defined by such behavioral symptoms as use of the words, "we" or "our," and the possible symptoms: resistance to leaving the group, pride in one's group, and acceptance of group goals.

The group referred to in group processes, then, is not just a collection of individuals. A group is not achieved through the mechanical addition of person to person, nor is the group simply a matter of individuals being spatially close to each other. When people engage cooperatively in related activity or work toward a common goal, they *create* a group. A group is a plurality of individuals, but what the group does is not plural, but singular.

The difficulty of accurately describing a group is inherent largely in the persistency of viewing the group as a collection, a plurality, rather than as a dynamic whole not only greater than the sum of its parts, but whose properties, such as its organization, its stability, its goals are something different from the properties of the individuals in it. A group of twelve persons is not twelve persons; it is a new quality. Individuals behaving as part of a group do not behave only as individuals. While it is possible to imagine a number of persons remaining in proximity who will not develop interrelations, no common activity or goal could have been introduced. The problem of group processes in many instances is the development of a group, where the behavior of members is interdependent and the members identify themselves with group goals and purposes.

Characteristics of an Effective Work Group

Groups are not all alike in their interdependency and identification. Cohesive groups possess natural internal relationships between members within the group and have certain distinguishing characteristics

---
[4] Kurt Lewin, "Field Theory and Experiment in Social Psychology," *American Journal of Sociology*, XLIV, May 1939, p. 868-96.

which, to some degree, are resident in all members of the group. Baxter and Cassidy have stated the characteristics of an effective work group somewhat as follows:

1. There is a "belongingness" in which all share. Persons within the group like to be together. Each is impelled to give of his best without restraint, without question as to how it will be received, and without undue introspection.
2. There is no reason for one individual to mistrust another. Each individual has a unique worth to himself and to the group. Both he and all other members are aware of this value. Each member has found his relationship to a common purpose. The bond which unifies individuals is, therefore, to be found in the group purposes.
3. There is an acceptance of a social control by the group. There is willingness, without effort, on the part of the members to trust majority decision and majority action. Not always of a unanimous nature, judgments of the group will not alienate completely any individual. Since true group decisions emerge without force and without pressure, every contributing person will have a part in shaping these decisions. Each will abide by the control which all have been instrumental in establishing.
4. The group which is characterized by unity of purposes, commonly held values and member-accepted control will have afforded to its members opportunities for becoming acquainted with one another, with each person's modes of thinking, individual habits of action, and needed satisfaction.[5]

Naturally all groups do not reach this stage of unity; it is the ideal toward which we must strive in our group life. Indeed, since every person is a member of several groups in our democracy, it becomes increasingly important that each individual should have experience in the processes through which group unification takes place. Do-Democracy is centered in the effective unification of problem-centered groups.

Process and Social Action—a Viewpoint

A group does not exist in a vacuum; it exists to act in terms of its needs, purposes, goals. If group processes are to be effective, the significance of processes and the value placed upon them become essential. In our hurrying to reach a goal processes have often been considered secondary to the end result and separated from ends. However, ends and means cannot be separated. To achieve democratic ends we must use democratic means.

There are a number of attitudes toward processes prevalent among individuals and groups today. Some say, "I don't care about red tape; I want results." These individuals and groups are so impatient for results, or have so little knowledge of the relation of means to ends,

---

[5] Bernice Baxter and Rosalind Cassidy, *Group Experience*. New York: Harper and Brothers, 1943. p. 20-21.

that they will not or cannot give proper attention to processes. Miel describes this group thus:

"They believe that if they have a well defined goal there is no reason why they should not aim directly at it—or as often happens, order some other persons to proceed at once toward the goal—without thought of the appropriateness of the means employed."[6]

Others shrug their shoulders, convinced of the futility of trying to direct social change and say, "What's the use?" They are unwilling to find a process, afraid to move from the status quo into the land of flexibility. A cynical group looks askance at process as a bag of tricks which enables the clique to gain its own ends no matter what the effect on others, and queries, "What's up your sleeve?" Finally, there are those who quite legitimately are distrustful of process because it has been used for its own sake. Process for the sake of process, the exploitation of process isolated from ends, leads the group to ask: "What does it accomplish? Where are the results?"

All of these groups have a misconception of process. Process is a means-end continuum. Ends and means go on interacting at all times; means become ends and ends become means toward other ends as the process continues. To be effective this process of interacting means and ends requires that equal attention be given to both. The goals continuously motivating the behavior of democratic peoples are long-time directional process goals; they lie in the way groups and individuals determine and achieve their purposes. The *end* is included in the *means* and the quality of an end can never rise above the quality of the means. Thus directional process goals assume superiority over fixed-end goals where no consideration is given to the way in which the goal is reached.

Efficient processes must be consistent with the ends they are intended to serve. Democratic ends are not achieved by autocratic means nor are dictatorial aims furthered by democratic procedures. The means of the democratic process are not learned in situations where the outcomes are arbitrarily determined in advance; nor can other useful skills of democratic action be learned in groups when purposes rest upon arbitrary external authority. Certainly much that passes for democratic process is a hybrid type which creates the illusion that people are achieving goals by democratic means; whereas, in reality, they are going through the motions and doing things which someone else has decided they should do. Where true democratic means function, the actual purposes of the

---

[6] Alice Miel. *Changing the Curriculum.* New York: D. Appleton-Century Company, 1946. p. 20.

group are changed by the process. In pseudo-democratic procedures, purposes remain fixed by outside authority while the group goes through the motions because it looks democratic.

As Miel points out, the process itself must contain guarantees: (a) of security, (b) of individual and group growth, and (c) of accomplishment if it is to be judged sound and adequate.[7] A major question we all face is whether we can learn to gain security through the processes used to bring social change under control. If there is no security in the processes, there will always be a retreat to old securities—recitations, lectures, texts, courses of study. A surer means of dealing with the novel aspects of life must be derived so that security may evolve in the process of control rather than on the assumption that change is evil or that preexisting permanence controls the essence of goodness. Dewey makes a plea for security in process when he says,

". . . there are a steadily increasing number of persons who find security in methods of inquiry, of observation, of experiment, of forming and following working hypotheses. Such persons are not unsettled by the upsetting of any special belief, because they retain security of procedure."[8]

Processes must result in growth of the persons participating. Desired growth "consists of increasing identification of self-interest with the interests of an ever-enlarging group."[9] Simply stated this means that certain egocentric tendencies of individuals must be turned to the service of others; instead of valuing achievement as a means of personal aggrandizement, it must be valued for its contribution to the common welfare. Individual and group growth in processes results in a neat balancing of an ambivalent social pull: (a) individuation—growth from dependence on others to self-dependencies; (b) democratic socialization—growth from absorption in self to concern for others.

As a final guarantee, effective processes must be productive. A process is judged by its products. Ends and means are parts of the whole. As individuals and groups proceed there must be evidence of progress. Individual and group purposes must be achieved.

Description of the Group Process

Group process as conceived in the light of the previous discussion *refers to the ends-means procedures utilized by a group of individuals thinking, discussing, planning, deciding, acting, and evaluating together*

---

[7] Miel, *op cit.*, p. 21-24.
[8] John Dewey, *The New Republic*, February 6, 1924; cited in John T. Childs, *Education and the Philosophy of Experimentalism*. New York: Century Company, 1931, p. 44.
[9] Miel, *op. cit.*, p. 24.

for the purpose of attacking and solving a common problem. It implies the meeting and interacting of minds in face-to-face relationships in which cooperative and creative thinking takes place and action and growth ensue. *The goal of group processes is group productivity, that is, getting something done which could not be done by a single individual.*

The real focus of group processes in education is relationships with or between people—pupil-pupil, teacher-pupil, teacher-teacher, and teacher-supervisor. The process creates and recreates designs which make the most of the collective judgments of the group members. The continuous mobilization of the positive elements which come out of the interaction of group members gives the group process its dynamic force and power. Its materials are the ideas, feeling, and experiences of people because the group *is* people. Group processes are simply the ends-means procedures developed by a group unified by interdependency of behavior and by the identification of the members with the group in attacking a common problem.

Characteristics of Group Processes

Processes are the ways we do things, the approaches we take, and the steps we follow as we seek to reach our goals. The *way* activity is carried on is as important if not more important than the activity itself. The characteristics of group processes fundamental to effective use can be briefly stated:

Group Atmosphere Is Democratic

Group atmosphere refers to the *basic feeling tone and emotional rhythm* which underlies the life of a group, the sum total of everybody's emotions toward each other, toward work and organization, toward the group as a unit, and toward things outside.[10] Democratic group process occurs when there is a permissive, democratic, experimental atmosphere as opposed to a punitive, hostile, competitive, autocratic climate. The amount of success a group has in achieving its goals is dependent not only on skills of group action but also on the atmosphere created in the group.

Lewin and his associates have conducted a series of "action-research" experiments on the interactions of individuals in three experimentally created social climates—authoritarian, democratic, and laissez-faire. The

---

[10] Fritz Redl and George Sheviakov, *Discipline for Today's Children and Youth.* Washington: NEA, Department of Supervision and Curriculum Development, 1944. p. 48.

findings seem to show quite clearly that a democratic social climate was more conducive to group productivity than either of the other climates.[11] Among the very significant differences between an autocratic and democratic group climate revealed were the following:

1. In the autocratic group, the leader was *above* the group; in the democratic, the leader was *in* the group; in the laissez-faire, the leader was *apart* from the group.
2. In moving toward goals, for the democratic group many paths are open; for the autocratic group there is only one—namely, that determined by the leader.
3. Differences in atmosphere affected group life, particularly interpersonal relations. There was thirty times as much hostile domination in autocratic atmosphere, more demands for attention, and more hostile criticism; in a democratic atmosphere cooperation and praise of the other fellow were more frequent, as were constructive suggestions and matter-of-fact behavior of member to member.
4. Group morale was decidedly higher in a democratic atmosphere. There was a higher degree of "we-centeredness," less "I-centeredness," and less conflict between members.
5. In a democratic atmosphere the group members did not show verbal aggression toward the leader nor try to make their social status more secure by winning his favor.
6. The democratic members remained more accessible to personal-social approaches from the leader.
7. Work in the democratic atmosphere was not interfered with by competing personal goals as it was in the authoritarian climate.
8. No need for release of hostility toward any member was apparent in the democratic climate, whereas two scapegoats were features of the authoritarian group.
9. The feeling of group belongingness and pride in the group products was much stronger in the democratic than in the authoritarian climate.
10. More creative and constructive work products emerged from the higher unity of the democratic climate with its greater amount of objectivity and cooperativeness of interpersonal relationships. In the democratic atmosphere there was a much higher acceptance of group goals, less conflict between cooperative group goals and individual ego goals, more goal setting by the group, and higher group productivity.[12]

Everyone Participates Voluntarily

Free interplay of minds and maximum use of individual potentials are essential. Every member of a democratic group must be guaranteed the right to have a direct voice in group purposing, thinking, discussing, planning, deciding, acting, and evaluating. Participation requires that each do his part for the sake of the general welfare. Each

---

[11] Kurt Lewin, Ronald Lippitt, and Ralph K. White, "Patterns of Aggressive Behavior in Experimentally Created Social Climates," *Journal of Social Psychology*, X, May 1939. p. 271-99.
[12] Ronald Lippitt, *An Experimental Study of the Effect of Democratic and Authoritarian Group Atmospheres.* Bulletin 16, No. 3. Iowa City: University of Iowa Studies in Child Welfare, 1940. p. 43-195. See also Ronald Lippitt and Ralph White, "The Social Climate of Children's Groups" in Roger G. Barker, Jacob S. Kounin, and Herbert F. Wright, *Child Behavior and Development.* New York: McGraw-Hill, 1943. p. 485-506.

group is made up of people with varying abilities, experiences, and personalities. All this member potential must be used if the group would accomplish that which an individual could not do. Indeed, participation alone makes the sum greater than its parts, for if I give you a dollar and you give me a dollar we shall each have a dollar. But if I give you an idea and you give me an idea, we shall each have two ideas!

All Action Is Cooperative

In developing ends-means procedures while attacking a common problem democratic cooperation is of paramount importance. Group power resides in the "co-active power" to work together on the highest level possible. Men have been working together since time immemorial, but the level of cooperation has not always been democratic. Cooperation, which literally means working together, is not one thing, but many. There are many levels of cooperation. Group processes must move from the low levels of cooperation such as compulsion, compromise, exploitation, or bargaining to the effective utilization of democratic cooperation where members of a group work together for a purpose, with the knowledge that in such a purpose each will find his highest realization.

In democratic cooperation group unity is gained through the formulation and acceptance of group goals. Goals are thought through and discussed, plans made, decisions reached, and action delegated by the group. Each individual voluntarily accepts responsibility for executing some part of the plan, yet he carries full responsibility for group achievement. Leadership and followership reside in each individual and the success or failure of the group purpose is determined by how well each person performs these functions. Through the mobilization of the best thinking of many, a democratic cooperating group can solve problems that the most gifted individual cannot begin to attack alone.

There Is Interaction among Members

Group processes facilitate intercommunication between members and between the group and its environment. Interaction means action between or among people or between groups. As there are levels of cooperation, so are there qualities of interaction. Democratic interaction in group processes means, above all, that the purposes, means, directions, actions, and evaluations evolve from the group as a result of man-to-man relationships and are not controlled by external authority. It means further that purposes are set by the group after inquiry into the needs of the individuals who compromise it. Each individual works with every other individual by sharing and evaluating individual experiences toward commonly accepted goals; each group works with every other group by isolating common needs, studying all data for their satisfaction, and agreeing on the most fruitful ways of achieving a desired goal.

It means that in attacking all problems each group member shall be free to study the conditions, state his viewpoints, and propose his solutions without fear of ridicule, violence, or suppression. Finally, it means that there is no end of inquiry fixed in advance by any thing or person—mores, customs, institutions, or persons with status authority. In its simplest terms, interaction means the fostering of good human relationships; the greater respect each individual has for others in a common effort, the higher the quality of interaction.[13]

The Group Formulates Goals

A salient point in group processes is the determination of objectives within the group. Groups do not exist without goals; a group is never just "doing nothing." Group goals are as real as individual goals.

The extent to which group goals command the concerted activity of members is dependent on the strength of the feeling of belongingness to the group and on whether or not goal setting is a part of the group process. In democratic group processes the goals are set by the group itself. The motivational value of self-set goals is infinitely greater than that of externally imposed goals. Group growth is stunted when the group works on problems that seem significant only to status leaders. When the group sets its own goals, the group starts where its members are and not where someone else thinks they should be.

Group processes, then, emphasize the well-known, but seldom practiced, adage, "Start where they are" and adds, "Go no faster than they are ready to go." Furthermore, it abandons that philosophy which says, "Well, we've set our objectives, so we've got to finish the job." Group goals in democratic group process are "open-ended" and flexibly held, for no group can have a clear vision of the final form which it wants solutions to take. Goals must not impose unnecessary limitations. They must be constantly redefined in terms of the end in view and the steps taken toward the goal must be continuously evaluated. It is good process to change goals; poor process to adhere to goals that bind and limit all efforts.

Every Group Member Is a "Change-Agent"

Each member of the group seeks to influence other people, to recog-

---

[13] The viewpoint here expressed is based on that expressed by L. Thomas Hopkins, *Interaction: The Democratic Process.* New York: D. C. Heath and Company, 1941, 490 p.

nize their needs for change, to diagnose needs in terms of the action required to meet them, to involve others as needed in effecting change, to plan appropriate action, to evaluate results of action according to plan, and to replan. Actually in any genuine process the "changer," individual or group, is also very much a "changee." The "changee," individual or group, gradually becomes an active "changer." The experimental attitude of democratic group processes requires an acceptance of the continuing necessity for changes in ways of thinking and behaving on the part of each member. Democratic group processes in thus accepting change must be seen for what they really are—a type of social change, a change in people—in their desires, beliefs, and attitudes, and in their understandings and skills.

All learning is goal-seeking behavior. When a group has (a) a desire to reach some goal, and (b) a realization that because of certain difficulties new and different ways of acting are required; effective group processes result in the group becoming a "change-agent." New understandings, skills, and attitudes are learned. Such learning involves *changes in* behavior. Indeed, maintenance and spread of changes in behavior is one of the concerns of group processes. To be effective as a member of a group each member, then, must be a "change-agent"; that is, he must act to produce changes in behavior of the group and its members in learning situations.

Group Morale and Discipline Are "We-Centered"

Group morale refers to the condition of a group where there are clear group goals accepted and integrated with individual goals; where there is confidence in the means of attainment, in the leadership, in the members, and in each member by himself; where actions are integrated and cooperative; and where aggression and hostility are expressed against forces frustrating the group rather than toward group members. As a psychological condition conducive to coordinated purposive activity it is the complex resultant of the strength of three forces: (a) forces that bind the members to a common goal; (b) forces that bind the members to their leadership; (c) forces that bind the members to themselves. Group discipline involves control of impulses of individuals composing the group for the attainment of a group goal; it is self-direction, a self-discipline based on understanding of the goal in view.

Two factors which greatly contribute to group morale and discipline are (a) the emotional security and satisfaction of the basic human need resulting from "belonging" in a group; and (b) the shift from "me" to "we"—the development of spontaneous cohesion in a group by working together for common goals, by accepting cooperative group goals as of greater concern than individual ego goals. In short, by thinking in terms of "we" rather than "I" and centering aims in common welfare more than in oneself.

Leadership Is a Function of the Group

Leadership in group processes is not a function of position; it evolves from the group, thus giving the responsibility for the selection of leadership to the group members. Each individual is a leader and a follower in group processes; leadership will reside first in one person and then in another. If a group functions in a democratic manner its dominant purpose will be to utilize for the group the best that everyone has to offer. In order to do this there can be no leadership solely by the "elite." Leadership is where you find it and authority resulting from leadership is something with which one *ends,* not *begins.*

Accordingly, leadership emerges anew as persons in different capacities and with different abilities learn to work together and as responsibility of different kinds is placed on different shoulders. Whatever authority a leader may have is authority along with rather than over others; it is derived from group consensus and voluntary choice of action rather than from fiat or decree. In short, leadership emerges from and is in the group; it does not originate outside the group.

Of all the characteristics of group processes presented above, perhaps the most important is that of cooperative action. This is the most efficient means of solving problems in a democracy. Six levels of cooperation have been identified by Courtis: *compulsion,* in which one individual works with another doing as he is bid because he is compelled against his will by force or fear; *compromise,* in which two parties, each unable to control the other, combine forces on some plan which represents a solution satisfactory to both, a solution which demands that each party to it give up something that was desired to obtain something considered essential; *exploitation,* in which through trickery one gets another to serve his purposes, as in the fable of the monkey, the cat, and the chestnuts; *bargaining,* in which each, for a price, gives the other what he wants; *leadership,* in which others follow a social-minded leader who has a vision for their welfare; and *democratic cooperation,* in which members of a socially-minded group work together for a common good, with the knowledge that in such a purpose each will find his highest self-realization.[14]

---

[14] National Education Association, Department of Supervisors and Directors of Instruction, *Teachers and Cooperation.* Washington: The Department, 1937. p. 7-9.

Much of what many people mean by cooperation never moves beyond the level of bargaining. In fact, much of the cooperation of the world is carried out on this level. Needless to say much school work proceeds on the lowest basis, compulsion. Compulsion, compromise, and exploitation have as emotional concomitants suspicion, hatred, a feeling of unfairness, and a spirit of revenge. Cooperation ceases on these levels as soon as the compelling force has been released. Group unity is never achieved; individuals are set against each other. Groups are pitted against groups. These lower levels of cooperation are divisive.

On the other hand, bargaining is individualistic; each acts for himself and there is no social unity except at the time of exchange. Leadership is weak in that the formulation of purposes, plans, and actions rest in the hands of the elite. It is not democratic, but autocratic, for the *few* purpose and plan, and the *many* act. If group processes are to be democratic, it is obvious that the level of cooperation which must characterize it is the democratic level where the group achieves unity through the participation of all and the cooperation of all in working on a common problem.

Analysis of Group Processes

Effective group processes demand the use of some general know-how or techniques of group dynamics in formulating ends-means procedures which take account of differences in groups and which are applicable to any process of group formation and development. For purposes of clarification in our thinking it is sound to analyze all that is involved in group processes as a base for the development of techniques. A description of group processes in terms of a "sequence of events" may leave the impression that several mutually exclusive steps are taken in logical order whenever group processes are functioning. Such is not the case. Group processes are continuous and cyclical.

In the literature there are few analyses of group processes. Two of the more recent ones are those by Baxter and Cassidy in *Group Experiences* and by Miel in *Changing the Curriculum*. Baxter and Cassidy make the following analysis of group processes:

Reason for coming together—goal or goals—general or specific

Actual assemblage—an aggregate of separate individuals—a positive or negative "emotional climate"

Planning—Defining goal or goals:

    Relation of one to another in terms of assigned tasks—division of labor

    Autocratic or democratic methods of the leader in clarifying purpose and assigning tasks

Weighted responsibility of the leader or leaders

When purpose is fully shared and individuals feel a sharing or "we-ness" or personal investment, then the cohesion is present which is essential for a group in the true sense of its meaning

Undertaking—process of practicing cooperative or uncooperative behavior—this shows the individual's ability to carry though an accepted task

Completion of plans, evaluation of outcomes in terms of goals— followed by replanning for the next undertakings.[15]

Miel points out that the requisites of group processes are (a) a meeting of people for the purpose of securing a meeting of minds; (b) discussion techniques which will bring in new facts, ideas, beliefs, and attitudes, and expose prejudices as well as change moods; (c) techniques of decision making, involving group planning; (d) division of labor so as to use special abilities residing in the group; (e) record-keeping of the thinking and action by groups.[16]

The following analysis of group processes is intended to indicate what a group needs to do to achieve productivity in attacking a problem. It is not intended to indicate steps or a logical sequence of events, but to provide a base for the development of techniques. To achieve maximum effectiveness with democratic group processes, a group needs:

- *Group thinking*—to think creatively as a group. A group does not think or rationalize as individuals think or rationalize. But thinking is done by the members of the group and the product of such thinking may be called "group thinking." This does not mean that the group thinks literally, but rather that it does know how to pool the concurrent result of creative individual thinking.
- *Group discussion*—to carry on group discussion so that its purpose becomes that of (a) understanding the other fellow's point of view instead of trying to argue or debate it; (b) harmonizing conflicts and integrating differences; (c) finding more useful ideas than the individuals alone bring to any group meeting.
- *Group planning*—to plan as a group so that (a) there is an identification of problems and clarification of goals; (b) consideration of the ends-means procedures for the attainment of these goals as efficiently as possible. A group plans intelligently when the members come to agreement on common goals and direct concerted action to their attainment.
- *Group decision*—to reach a group decision cooperatively. Action demands decision. Periods of creative thinking, discussing and planning usually produce a wealth of suggestions, but before action can be taken there must be a selection of the plan of action. This calls for group decision.
- *Group action*—to act democratically as a group so that each member does his part in carrying out as effectively as possible the decisions of the group. Democratic group action, when fully understood, is far more efficient than autocracy, but it must be "caught and taught."

---

[15] Baxter and Cassidy, *op. cit.*, p. 52-53.
[16] Miel, *op. cit.*, p. 134-41.

- **Group evaluation**—to evaluate not only the productivity of the group, but the very processes by which the group achieved its goals. Group evaluation is concerned with (a) the evaluation of leadership; (b) the evaluation of the group processes; (c) the evaluation of changes brought about in persons; and (d) the evaluation of group action in terms of the values embedded in group purposes.

As one reads this bulletin no doubt he is thinking: "Well, all this is very fine. But *how* do we do it? What are the steps in group processes? Where do we start? What is the sequence of events."

Our problem is this: Can we learn to use group processes as (a) a learning process; (b) a means of problem-solving; (c) a democratic experience? Learning implies some sequence of events—some steps in group processes. However, there is no formula, no set pattern for group processes. The experiences of those who participated in the Second Annual Meeting of the Association for Supervision and Curriculum Development in Chicago[17] March 1947, as well as of those who were members of the First National Training Laboratory on Group Development,[18] both of which were efforts to attack problems by means of group processes, clearly reveal that there is no one pattern for group processes.

Group processes function in a total situation. Every situation which a group faces is different. Hence, there can be no single pattern for group processes. Effective group processes can be evolved only for a particular situation. To those who find security in formulas, in logical one, two, three, four sequence this means that security must be found in the processes themselves. A process that contains guarantees of security, of individual and group growth, and of accomplishment cannot be automatic. The processes are dependent upon the nature of the group, its purposes, means, obstacles, ends. In short, adequate group processes meet the situation as the group finds it and are effective if they work in developing means-ends procedures which enable a particular group to achieve its goals.

Group Thinking and Discussing

Group thinking means group intelligence in operating—that is, the group possesses the ability and disposition to agree on group goals and to work out means for their accomplishment. An intelligent group when it faces a problem, just like an intelligent individual, selects, defines,

---

[17] National Education Association, Association for Supervision and Curriculum Development. *Report on the Second Annual Meeting of Association for Supervision and Curriculum Development, March 23-26.* Washington: The Association for Supervision and Curriculum Development, 1947. 84 p. (Planographed)

[18] National Education Association and Research Center for Group Dynamics, MIT. *First National Training Laboratory on Group Development.* Bethel, Maine. 1947 (Mimeographed)

delimits, and clarifies a specific problem with sharpness and clearness through group thinking.

It is as simple as asking the three basic questions suggested by de Huszar: (a) *What* is it?—defining the problem; (b) *How* do we deal with it?—deciding upon ends-means procedures; (c) *Who* shall do what?[19] Group thinking, in answering such questions, must unalterably lead to action. Group thinking is essential today, for modern life is full of problems too complex and interdependent to be attacked through skills and knowledges carried in "one small head." As Howard Lane points out, "Man cannot think clearly alone; he requires the checks and balances of other men and normally seeks conference and counsel when it is his purpose to know the truth, to act in accord with wider wisdom." [20]

In the beginning of group processes perhaps the greatest hurdle is moving from an inventory of problems or a "problem census" to the identification and analysis of *a* problem. A group must decide on a specific statement of a unitary problem. Only one problem can be undertaken at a time. In the initial stages of problem identification and analysis creative group thinking emerges from group discussion. In the process of group discussion, individuals learn how to contribute effectively to the thinking of the group and to incorporate the ideas of others into their thinking. And what is more important, each achieves a "sense of belonging" through having participated and having been of service to the group; each shares his experiences with others, and there is co-creating in the group through the discovery of new relationships and the synthesizing of experience.

Some Characteristics of Effective Group Discussion

Effective group thinking and discussion get individual personalities expressed in terms of the group. Some of the characteristics of effective discussion are:

Group members participate freely in discussion; the "atmosphere" of the group is permissive, cooperative, democratic.

Leadership is assumed by various members of the group and passes from one to another as various aspects of the problem are considered.

Questions stimulate group thinking.

Facts, experiences, and opinions are given as they contribute to the clarification and attack of the problem.

Illustrations are given to make points clear.

---

[19] de Huszar, *op. cit.,* p 37.
[20] Howard Lane, "Education for Social Intelligence," *Group Planning in Education.* 1945 Yearbook, National Education Association, Department of Supervision and Curriculum Development. Washington: The Department, 1945. p. 4.

Erroneous and irrelevant statements are used to throw light on the problem.

Terms whose meanings become doubtful or a matter of dispute are carefully defined in words the group understands.

Statements of group members are clarified when this is needed to give them meaning to the entire group.

Problems are restated when a revision of them is necessary or when a restatement helps focus attention on central ideas of discussion.

A statement is not accepted as "fact" because a certain person makes it unless the person by virtue of study is qualified to speak as an authority and can support the statement with proof.

Summaries are made to help focus attention on what has been accomplished.

Important ideas which hold promise of advancing the discussion are centered upon when they occur in order that the group may be challenged to see their relevancy to the problem before it.

Discussion is brought to a close in a way that is designed to make evident what has been accomplished and what is further suggested.

There is evidence that the members of the group have a sense of achieving the purpose which directs discussion.

Techniques of Group Thinking and Discussion

The literature of group action is well stocked with general suggestions for group discussion, but there are few suggestions which are organized in terms of specific techniques and procedures. The suggestions for participating in cooperative thinking through group discussion which were prepared for the Michigan Study in Secondary School Curriculum are specific "hows" of group thinking and discussion.

1. Each person should do his own thinking. Don't try "to save time" by telling the group the right answer. The leader is not a group instructor, but a social engineer, trying to arrange conditions so that each will do creative thinking.
2. Group discussion is not a debating society. We do not argue for the fun of it. The issues are of great importance; wise men disagree in their views; our task is to find more truth than we bring to any group meeting. We are in a cooperative quest. Our thinking is creative rather than combative.
3. Ask yourself which ideas, experiences, and differences are basic, fundamental, and most worth discussing.
4. When discussion wanders, restate the question and get a new start. Sometimes, if the side-line is especially important, put it up to the group, "Shall we follow this interesting issue that has come up, or shall we return to the plan of discussion originally adopted?"
5. Make short statements, not speeches.
6. Do not pass any important matter that is not clear to you. Sometimes individuals hear unfamiliar terms and assume that everyone else must understand; hence they fear it would be humiliating to ask for explanations or illustrations. This is untrue. Have you not often been glad when someone else asked for clarification on a point on which you had been none too clear? Others may profit too, but you are in the group to learn, and you must not hesitate to ask.

7. If you find yourself talking more than other members of the group, train yourself to pass over minor points and to speak on only a few carefully chosen issues.
8. Use special care to be fair to positions represented by a minority or not represented at all in the group. If you are aware of a position not being adequately represented, present it as its adherents would like to hear it stated, then explain your disagreement.
9. Challenge contributions you cannot fully accept. Do not keep your disagreements quiet in the mistaken notion that it is better manners to pretend to agree when you do not. Make inquiry concerning the assumptions involved in the contribution.
10. The "either-or" attitude is on the whole not fruitful. Search rather for new means which enable both sets of values to be pursued without clash. Our concern in cooperative thinking is not simply to choose between two ways we now know, but if possible to find a way of integrating the values of both, thereby creating an improved solution. However, avoid smoothing over differences. Differences should be probed with questions to make them clear and sharp.
11. When there is some confusion over a diversity of opinions expressed, a minute of silence can do much to help members rise to a clearer perspective of what has been said. In suggesting this pause the chairman should restate the precise issue under discussion. After the pause the members may be more able to cooperate in detecting the root of the disagreements. This may be in the partial nature of the experience and evidence used, or in a difference in the sense of values. Try to keep in mind some ends everyone wants.
12. Be on the lookout for different uses of the same word. Call for illustrations whenever this difference becomes confusing. Do not wrangle over a verbal definition.
13. Trust the group. There is no person in it who is not superior to the rest in at least one respect. The experience of all is richer than the experience of any. The group as a whole can see further and more truly than its best member. Remember that every member of the group is an individual just as you are.
14. For every discussion there is available a limited amount of time. Each individual should help make it possible to utilize the time more effectively. To attempt too much in too short a time fosters a habit of slipshod and superficial thinking.
15. Summarize (a) whenever a major point is finished before going on to the next; (b) whenever the discussion has been fairly long and drawn out or confused; (c) shortly before the close of the period. Try to use the words of members of the group rather than your translation.[21]

Group Planning and Decision

Group thinking and discussion must lead to plans and decisions. To stop short of planning and decision is to render the processes sterile, for no product is achieved. The job of thinking together is not an easy one, we grant, but group intelligence can convert desires into plans. Out of group thinking and discussion must emerge a method, a know-how, so as to translate decisions into plans for action. In short, group planning

---

[21] J. Cecil Parker, "Some Suggestions for Participating in Cooperative Thinking Through Group Discussion" in Miel, *op cit.*, Appendix D. Also in A. S. Barr, William H. Burton, Leo J. Brueckner, *Supervision.* New York: Appleton-Century Company, 1947. p. 97.

answers the question, *How* do we do it? It is simply the conscious and deliberate guidance of group thinking and discussion so as to create logical ends-means procedures for achieving agreed-upon group goals. Group planning assumes that it is possible for us to anticipate, predict, guide, and control our group destiny; it implies a pragmatic realism as contrasted to fatalism.

Group planning and decision involve the following fundamental steps: (a) the clear definition of the problem during a period of group thinking and discussion and the formulation of real group goals; (b) the selection of possible paths of action (ends-means) toward the goals; (c) the election of a path of action (group decision) and the application of the action to the problem.

In reality group planning is closely akin to problem-solving. Indeed, the steps in group planning are much the same as the steps in problem-solving, for would we plan if we didn't face the problem of making our actions move toward our goals?

Some Principles of Group Planning [22]

How do you begin group planning? The secret of group planning is to be found in practice. We learn to plan by planning. Group planning can not be put into a neat formula of things to be done and not to be done. When group planning begins, experience shows that it is most effective when consideration is given by the group to certain conditions and principles. These are:

Everyone is in on it. The planning gives opportunity and encourages *all* members of the group who will be directly affected by the results of the planning to participate and share in the thinking.

Planning should grow out of the expressed needs and interests of the members who compose the group. The basis for planning should be the group goals rather than those imposed by one.

Planning gives scope to individual interests and an opportunity to "belong." The final determination of the problem is broad enough to include the real interests of all members of the group so that each may "belong," that is, have status in and recognition by the group.

Planning must have an adequate factual basis. It calls for the use of critical thinking and the scientific method in the search for truth. Plans are "reality based" to the extent that they are based on facts.

The most effective plans come out of a process which combines continuous planning and evaluation. As the work progresses changes are made as the actual work proves them necessary. The planning leads to

---

[22] Adapted from Harleigh Trecker, *The Group Process in Administration.* New York: The Woman's Press, 1946. p. 77-79; and H. H. Giles in *Group Planning in Education,* 1945 Yearbook. National Education Association, Department of Supervision and Curriculum Development. Washington: The Department, 1945. p. 142-43.

continuity, to more seeking, learning, and evaluating, to changing behavior continuously to meet new situations.

The planning itself and the things planned are flexible and "open-ended." There is provision for the group to re-think its purposes and procedures and to state new ideas frankly. The sequence of events in group planning is *not* Herbartian, not seriatim. Goals change and ends and means change as experience directs.

Group planning results in "collective self-control" for the sake of group goals; it does not inevitably result in someone's telling someone else what to do.

The most effective plans grow out of a process that is often slow, and seemingly drawn out. Group members are patient with the process. Those who cry "action" not "more paper plans" can speed up the realization of plans without planning to do so. The "doer" must also be a "planner."

The planning uses all available resources of the environment which are pertinent to the problem. Furthermore, planning makes use of existing plans and resources rather than starting from scratch with every new problem. We build on what we have, provided it is useful and furnishes a foundation for the problem.

Planning requires documentation and record-keeping. The results of group thinking, discussing, planning, deciding, acting, and evaluating must be preserved to provide continuity and direction. Records must be available for purposes of summary and evaluation.

Planning provides means for recognizing the contributions of all to group goals. Each individual grows with self-confidence in his ability to contribute. Hence group members should receive recognition for their help.

Planning gives order and shape to group experiences. It enables the group to do things in an orderly way, to think before action, and to act in the light of facts rather than guesses.

Group planning is not power based. The group does not plan under the influence of the majority or minority in the group or outside the group. It plans in terms of cooperative action and the mutual acceptance by all of the group goals.

Techniques of Group Planning

Effective group planning is particularized in terms of the differences in the situations which the group meets. There is no one pattern for group planning; each group makes its own plan and may never use the identical procedures a second time, for group goals are always changing. Group planning, however, requires some fundamental skills involved in problem-solving. The "steps" in group planning seem to proceed like this:

- The group defines the problem and formulates its goals.
- The group analyzes the problem to discover (a) causes of dissatisfaction; (b) relationship of causes to consequences; (c) relation of all elements to consequences: materials, change-agents, tools, sequences; and (d) values attached to all elements and consequences.

- The group decides what standards of value shall control the selection of possible paths of action.
- The group collects all data and ideas pertinent to attacking the problem.
- The group classifies the collection of data in terms of (a) selected standards of value; (b) defined purposes.
- The group selects the most pertinent paths of action (ends-means procedures), thus forming a connected sequence of events from the present situation to the desired goals. It allows plenty of time for pooling of facts and harmonizing of conflicts.

Group Decision

After the group has formulated several paths of action, it must select specific action. This involves group decision as to (a) deciding *how* to do it and (b) deciding *who* should do what. In striving for group decision regarding a possible course of action the group acts cooperatively. The decision as to final plans for action should be the result of the decision of the group after careful study of the probable outcomes.

We know little about the techniques of arriving at group decision, but "action-research" has pointed out the necessity for coming to a group decision. We must be careful to distinguish between discussion and decision. Group discussion and group planning may assist in clarifying issues and bringing about motivation in the desired direction. Motivation alone, however, does not suffice to lead to change. To be motivated is one thing, to transform motivation into concrete goals and to stabilize these goals in a way which would carry the group beyond discussion and planning to the actual completion of the work is another.

Controlled experiments have been made by Lewin [23] with groups of housewives, and by Willerman [24] with students' cooperatives. Comparisons were made of the relative effectiveness of a lecture method and a method of group decision as a means of changing food habits. They show that discussion without group decision did not lead to as great a change in food habits as did discussion and group decision.

One reason why group decision facilities change is illustrated by Willerman's study of cooperatives. The students were to change from the consumption of white to whole wheat bread. When the change was simply requested, the degree of eagerness varied greatly with the degree of personal preference for whole wheat. After group decision, however, the eagerness to reach the group goal was relatively independent of per-

---

[23] Kurt Lewin, *The Relative Effectiveness of a Lecture Method and a Method of Group Decision for Changing Food Habits.* Bulletin No. 111. Washington: National Research Council, 1943. (Mimeographed)

[24] B. Willerman, *Group Decision and Request as a Means of Changing Food Habits.* Bulletin No. 108. Washington: National Research Council, 1943. p. 35-65.

sonal preference; the individual seemed to act mainly as a "group member." In short, group decision provides a background of motivation where the individual is ready to cooperate as a member of the group more or less independent of his personal inclinations.

In a similar study, Bavelas experimented with the effectiveness of group decision on production in a sewing factory. His study also revealed the superiority of group decision over pressure methods.[25]

The findings of "action-research" reported by Lewin which have implications for techniques of group decision are:

1. Group decisions in setting up production goals are more effective than pressure methods.
2. Discussion which leads to a *general* decision to increase production without setting *definite* production goals to be reached in a definite time is less effective than discussion which leads to specific decisions.
3. Discussions without decisions do not make for real participation by group members in group action.
4. Members of groups which *discuss* and *decide* tend to identify themselves with the decision of the group.
5. Group decision links motivation provided by group discussion and planning to action and, at the same time, seems to move change to a new level. This seems to be the reason that a process-like decision, which takes only a short time, is able to affect conduct for many months to come.
6. Decision in a group setting seems to be effective in enabling members, who will never see each other again, to carry out group goals.
7. To change group goals efficiently demands that the change-agent deal with the individual as a group member. Goals must be set for the group as a whole and for individuals in a group setting.
8. It is easier to change ideology or cultural habits by dealing with groups than with individuals. As long as group standards are unchanged, the individual will resist changes. However, if group standards are changed, the conflict between individual and group standards is eliminated.
9. The anchorage of the motivation of the individual in a group decision goes far in achieving the execution of the decision and in establishing certain self-regulatory processes on the new level of ideology and action.[26]

The significant implications of these findings for teachers, supervisors, and administrators seem to be: (a) group discussion and planning are not productive without group decision which sets up definite group goals; (b) group decision enables the individual group member to cooperate as a "group member" and to act in accordance with group goals instead of personal goals; (c) group decision links the motivation pro-

---

[25] Alex Bavelas, "The Effects of Group Decision in a Sewing Machine Factory," in Kurt Lewin, "Frontiers in Group Dynamics," *Human Relations*, Vol. 1, No. 1, 1947. p. 25.
[26] Kurt Lewin, "Dynamics of Group Action," *Educational Leadership*, I, January 1944, p. 195-200, and Lewin, "Frontiers in Group Dynamics," *op. cit.*, p. 35-38.

vided by group discussion and planning to group action; (d) changes in group goals occur only when the goals are set by the group; (e) group decision provides a "freezing" of motivation which results in the group member regulating his actions in accordance with the new level of ideology and action the group is seeking. It seems obvious that group decision is a crucial phase of effective group processes. Without group decision, group processes are short circuited.

Techniques of Group Decision

"Action-research" to date gives us few significant clues as to how to achieve group decision. We may, however, derive techniques of group decision from doing things democratically. Traditionally, group decision is arrived at by majority vote or through the operation of "parliamentary law." Unfortunately both these techniques of democracy are often individualistic and power based. For example, in arriving at group decision by means of parliamentary law, one makes a motion, another moves to amend, a third to lay on the table, a fourth to vote. Each individual tends to act as an individual, and not as a group member. His actions and suggestions for arriving at a decision are an effort to get the group to adopt his decision as the group decision. The group decision often becomes a forced *compromise* by means of majority vote. Such a compromise divides the group into a majority and a minority. Such a group decision does not represent cooperation on the most effective democratic level; it is cooperation by compromise.

Majority rule is one of the traditional techniques of democratic group decision. However, it is an inadequate technique in arriving at group decision. Indeed, one of the greatest restrictions on the effectiveness of group processes is the unwarranted assumption that the limit of social invention has been attained and that existing democratic techniques are sacred and are not to be tampered with by addition or subtraction. Democracy is an emerging concept and as it moves ahead new techniques must be developed and utilized to meet new situations. In the problem of group decision in education we cannot afford to be content with majority rule. We must move beyond all types of group decision which are devisive to those which unify.

In the most effective level of democratic group processes the group never makes a decision except by unanimous consent. Group decision is the result of a *consensus* in the action to be taken. Such consensus is best reached through active, responsible participation by all concerned with the consequences of action. Consensus, the arriving at unanimity, or practical unanimity, moves beyond majority voting in arriving at group decision. Group processes cannot be most effective when a majority coerces a minority.

To achieve consensus is not easy. It demands that all conflicts be harmonized before a decision is reached. We are too often impatient for decision; progress in arriving at a decision will be slower than some members of the group desire. Unanimous consent is costly in time to achieve, but it contributes greatly to the growth of group morale, group solidarity, and group productivity. Furthermore, consensus is impossible to achieve unless the group has grown in social awareness so that each member is group conscious and values the unity and productivity of group processes above the achievement of his own ego goals.

Consensus does not, on the other hand, rule out deviate contributions; i.e., devious from the current majority view. In striving for consensus, deviate contributions are not only permitted but also valued as possible improvements of the majority view and of the emerging consensus. Minorities as well as majorities have responsibilities as well as rights in the process of striving for consensus. All contribution should be directed toward a wider sharing and testing of available experiences in the attack on the problem and in suggesting possible courses of action. Contributions, which jeopardize group goals, must either be helped to conform or eventually be rejected.

There is often difficulty in achieving consensus because group allocation of responsibility to individuals or committees leaves some members of the group uninformed. The entire group must not only be informed constantly as to what sub-parts of the group are thinking and doing, but also must know that it can affect whatever is going on in subgroups. In other words, there must be constant interaction between the group as a whole and any sub-parts organized for the sake of efficiency.

The spirit with which one views consensus is of great importance. Consensus is most easily achieved if the group considers it in the scientific spirit of mind as a hypothesis, an action to be tested and tried. Any consensus reached is held experimentally and tested in action. Cooperative evaluation of the results of group decision in action is one phase of group processes. A group decision is never an absolute; if it is treated as such there will always be difficulty in getting a consensus of minds. A scientifically minded group when arriving at a group decision says, "Let's try it," not "Let's settle it once and for all."

Suggestions for Achieving Group Decision

In striving for consensus when arriving at a group decision, a group will find it helpful to proceed somewhat as follows:

- Give full opportunity for every member of the group to contribute every suggestion he feels is pertinent.
- Each member who does not understand a suggestion asks questions until he does. Allow plenty of time for pooling of facts and harmonizing of values.
- During the gathering of suggestions the leader holds all members to *understanding* of the various paths of action. The group refrains from criticism or comment; it seeks to gather and to understand. Where possible all suggestions should be listed on a blackboard and numbered. The process of collection and understanding proceeds until group creativity has been exhausted.
- Use a straw preferential vote to uncover minority opinion early in the process. Each member votes for each suggested path of action he thinks should be considered. The vote tabulation reveals any minority present.
- Seek for consensus by a full discussion of the minority point of view in an effort to harmonize conflicts of value and method. The minority group members state their objections with reasons as well as their suggestions as to how the majority goals or path of action may be modified to meet their objections. The *group as a whole* does its best by way of creative thinking and effort to modify the suggested goals and path of action favored by the majority until the goals and path of action become acceptable to the dissenting; in this way the conflict of each minority member is harmonized. When unanimity has been achieved through harmonization, the modified goals and courses of action become the group decision. Where the conflict is one of different methods, the group may often authorize both on an experimental basis.
- If after adequate discussion and efforts to harmonize conflicts a group is still fairly evenly divided as to path of action necessary to achieve a group goal, the group may well consider whether or not it is imperative to make a decision at the time. Often a "cooling off" period or a postponement of the decision until further study can be made by all group members may result in consensus at the next meeting.
- If all efforts to reach a consensus have bogged down, and some decision must be made in order to test the plan of action, appeal to the sportsmanship of the minority, but make it clear that the decision is a trial one, and not a final one unless it works so well as to satisfy all concerned.[27]

Group Action

Effective group action has three prime requisites: (a) a genuine interest in the group project; (b) a belief on the part of group members in each other and in the cooperative democratic process; and (c) a desire to make it work. Group action is oriented in Do-Democracy; there is something for each group member to do in the process of thinking, discussing, planning, deciding, acting, and evaluating. In participating in group

---

[27] Adapted from Miel, *op. cit.*, p. 139 and *Teachers and Cooperation*, p. 30-32.

action the individual subverts his own interests to the wishes of the group in situations requiring common action, and in accordance with the principles of democracy, he assumes his share in carrying out a group decision.

The one factor which restricts effective group action above all others is the attitude which so many share that democratic group action is not compatible with group efficiency. Many assume that democratic group action must move more slowly than autocratic action; that democracy must fumble in every crisis; and that inefficiency is the price of democratic group action. "Action-research" has produced evidence which challenges these assumptions. The experiments of Lewin, Lippitt, and others in the field of group dynamics have given us fresh evidence that democratic group action can be efficient.

Lippett's work, with experimentally created "social climates" in groups, quite sharply points out the superiority of democratic group action over authoritatian action. In comparing the productivity of two groups of boys' clubs in which the experimental factor was the social climate, democratic as opposed to autocratic, Lippitt found that (a) individual ego goals arose in the authoritarian group which conflicted with the group goals; (b) there was more "I-centeredness" and less "we-centeredness" in the authoritarian group; (c) the group goal was more potent as a determiner of action in the democratic group and the group products were more truly a collective possession; (d) more creative and constructive work products emerged from the democratic group with its greater amount of cooperativeness of interpersonal relations.[28] French also found a higher level of participation, we-feeling, motivation, and interdependence by all members in meeting group problems in his organized groups than in his unorganized groups.[29] The work of Lewin and Willerman on group decision, presented above, also points out the superiority of democratic group decision over lectures and requests. Bavelas found that as certain leaders went through a training process to carry out more democratic procedures of leadership, the groups improved both "in the efficiency of work organization" and "the quality and output of the work."[30]

There is an increasing amount of experimental data being made available by "action research" in group dynamics which indicates that demo-

---

[28] Ronald Lippitt. *An Experimental Study of the Effect of Democratic and Authoritarian Group Atmospheres.* Bulletin 16, No. 3. University of Iowa Study in Child Welfare, 1940. p. 43-195; 188-90.
[29] John R. P. French, Jr. "The Disruption and Cohesion of Groups," *Journal of Abnormal Social Psychology*, XXXVI, 1941. p. 361-78.
[30] Alex Bavelas, "Morale and the Training of Leaders," in *Civilian Morale*, (G. Watson, ed.) Boston: Houghton Mifflin, 1942. p. 143-65.

cratic group action is more efficient. Group action, however, to be effective, demands that the group members *learn* democratic ways of acting. As Lewin points out, "the change from autocracy to democracy takes more time than from democracy to autocracy. Autocracy is imposed on the individual; democracy has to be learned."[31] What do we know about the ways of democratic action? Not as much as we should, but we do know that:

1. Effective group action, or personal action based on group consensus, must arise out of a need felt by those participating—not out of a need imposed from above.
2. It is the responsibility of the group members to act upon group decisions.
3. Effective group action develops an intolerance of group pathologies such as: inability to arrive at a decision; failure to use member potential; inability to use resources; inability to evaluate success or failure of group processes; rigidity of organization; prevention of the assimilation of new members; rigidity of role structure; i.e., same people always leaders or followers; rigidity of procedure; lack of reality in goal setting; non-participation; inability to develop techniques for determining who is going to participate and when.
4. Group decision and group action are closely linked. One can't exist without the other. As a process of social change, democratic group decision links motivation and action.
5. It is easier to change the ways of acting of individuals formed into a democratic group than to change the ways of any one of them separately. Lewin says: "As long as group values are unchanged the individual will resist changes more strongly the further he is to depart from group standards. If the group standard itself is changed, the resistance which is due to the relation between individual and group standard is eliminated."[32] Hence to get democratic group action we must begin by changing group processes to realistic democratic group processes.
6. Democratic group action is more efficient in that (a) group purposes and goals represent the individual welfare and combined values of the members of the group—no person, policy, tradition, or pattern of loyalty to a chief or symbol takes precedence over the welfare of the individuals in a group; (b) group processes are constantly revised and evaluated within the group in terms of their effectiveness in achieving group goals; (c) group action liberates, develops, and uses the intelligence of every member of the group.

Suggestions for Improving the Effectiveness of Group Action

Group action means doing things democratically. The whole concept of group processes involves ends-means procedures for doing things democratically. Improving the effectiveness of group action stems from and depends upon improving the techniques of group thinking, discussing, planning, and evaluating. The group acts in accord with a foresight of human outcomes; it possesses skill and resources for predicting the social

---
[31] Kurt Lewin, "Experiments in Social Space," *Harvard Educational Review*, IX, January 1939. p. 31.
[32] Lewin, "Frontiers in Group Dynamics," *op. cit.*, p. 34.

outcomes of behavior. We learn by doing and, so in group processes, too, we learn to improve group action through participating in group processes. Experience and research have provided some clues for improving group action. These are:

The size of a group can be a barrier to effectiveness; as a group grows beyond thirty members, effective group action becomes increasingly difficult. A desirable size cannot be reached by arbitrarily setting up one figure, for function and make-up condition the most desirable size. A small group of ten to fifteen members is probably most efficient.

Physical settings must be conducive to group processes. The size and type of a room as well as physical arrangement within the room are important. For effective participation the group members must be able to hear and see each other; the seating arrangement must facilitate good human relations. De Huszar emphasizes the circle (round table) rather than the rectangle as the "formation of democratic togetherness."[33] A blackboard is useful.

The plan of action that emerges should be appraised to the end that individuals in the group receive their share of work to be done. In the final analysis, a group can act efficiently only through individuals. Responsibility for action should be delegated in terms of individual interests and abilities. A division of labor is not disruptive of cooperation.

Sufficient time must be allowed to insure a successful attack upon a problem and the development of action suggestions.

Consideration of group metabolism increases effectiveness. Fatigue, tension, tempo, pace, atmosphere affect group action. Within the process, provision for brief recesses and for adjusting the length of the meetings will result in more efficiency.

Within the process itself the most difficult step is moving from the problem inventory and identification to how and who. Usually it is not difficult for the group to say *what* the problem is, but it is more difficult to say *what* should be done about it; and it is easier to say what needs doing than to say *how* and *who*. Effective group action depends upon the *how* and *who*. A group must develop machinery especially for delegating group action—for determining *who*.

Individual Skills in Group Action

To achieve effective group action each individual must develop certain skills. A group member needs to (a) exercise initiative and accept responsibility for the group; (b) to be group conscious; (c) to regulate his thinking and action in terms of group goals; (d) to get rid of personal sensitivity to criticism; (e) to be keenly aware of the fact that the group will succeed or fail to the extent that he does his part and participates actively.

---
[33] de Huszar, *op. cit.*, p. 31.

S. A. Courtis offers some good suggestions for cooperating skillfully as a member of a group. An effective group member:

1. Adopts a social point of view. He thinks with the other fellow as well as for himself; he thinks for the group as a whole until he naturally says "we" instead of "I."
2. Acts as an *organ* of the group. He thinks, discusses, plans, decides, acts, evaluates on his own initiative and contributes whenever and as often as he has a contribution.
3. Regulates his thoughts, language, behavior, in terms of group purposes and procedures. He considers the probable effect of all he does and says upon fellow members and the group as a whole *before* he acts; and he evaluates the effects after he acts.
4. Is impersonal. After having presented his contribution, he gives up all sense of ownership of it; he never defends it, but *explains* it. He is unemotional about the way it is treated; he surrenders his contribution to the group and thereafter treats it as impersonally as if another had offered it.
5. Tries to understand the other fellow's point of view as well as his own. He puts himself in his place and tries to desire his objectives and think his thoughts and then consider how the group can help the other fellow.
6. Understands and holds to group purposes.
7. Believes that "each for all, all for each" is the ideal way to preserve the balance between individual and group goals.[34]

Insofar as each group member is expected to be a "change-agent" he must develop certain skills of social action if he is to participate in changing the understandings, attitudes, and performances of a group member and the group as a whole. The skills of social action, which a group member should develop in order to participate effectively as a group member, are primarily skills involved in: utilizing values as determiners of choice, thinking, communicating, working with others and being worked with, acquiring and maintaining an understanding of the world today.[35]

Group Evaluation

Group evaluation is continuous; it goes on in every part of the process. Very simply it is the answering of the question: How well have we done? The group looks back over what it has done and tries to find out how well it has performed. Group evaluative techniques are concerned with the following aspects of evaluation: (a) evaluation of leadership; (b) evaluation of the group process; (c) evaluation of outcomes or changes brought about in persons; and (d) evaluation of group action in terms of group goals.

The evaluation of the group process *per se* is essentially the study and review of operating experiences. It is an appraisal of the worth and

---

[34] *Teachers and Cooperation*, p. 35-36.
[35] J. Cecil Parker, "A Trend in Secondary School Curriculum," *California Journal of Secondary Education*, XXII, October 1947. p. 352-56.

productivity of all the ends-means procedures used by a group in moving toward goals. It implies a desire to measure results and to make changes in both goals and ends-means procedures as the result of evaluative evidences.

Basic Assumptions Underlying Group Evaluation

Evaluation is an important step in group processes; it is a function of the total situation rather than one of its particular parts.

Evaluation of group processes must be done in terms of the goals the group is attempting to achieve and the efficiency which the processes produce.

Evaluation emerges from the actual experiences of people working together, and evaluative techniques are formulated and executed through democratic methods.

The most effective evaluation is continuous rather than periodic. It accompanies every effort of the group and is founded in a desire to improve each situation without waiting for special evaluation periods.

The control of evaluation is held within the group which is trying to measure and evaluate. This helps the group improve the process in making the present group experience better and gives it the ability to direct subsequent group processes to even more productive levels.

Techniques of Group Evaluation

Each group should develop its own evaluative techniques to meet its particular situation. Among the techniques of merit are:

Evaluation sessions. Toward the end of each group meeting an evaluation session of approximately fifteen minutes may be held. The chairman or leader breaks off discussion and suggests to the group that it look back at its ways of working to see how it has functioned as a group and how its productivity may be increased. Such sessions serve to (a) deepen the group's insight into group processes; (b) develop plans for group processes which would make for greater productivity in later sessions.

Process observer reports. One or more group members may observe group processes for purposes of helping the group evaluate its own efforts. Such observers seek objectively to view group behavior and to record what happened in group processes and why it happened. Their records would contain such data as they could observe concerning: participation pattern, group direction (how it is set, changed, and maintained), group atmosphere (hostile, friendly, formal, matter of fact), use of resource persons, group action, and interesting group behavior.

Review of group records. Each group should keep a diary account of the development of its experiences. A secretary should keep a record of group thinking and action, of plans and decisions. The secretary should periodically summarize the group activities so as to keep the group on the track and give it a chance to review its progress.

Post-meeting ratings. Rating scales of productivity can be developed by each group, and at the end of each session group members can evaluate the meeting in terms of how they felt about the group's progress. A study of these post-meeting ratings is an excellent evaluation measure.

Growth As a Base for Evaluation

Although it is not possible to present a long list of criteria for evaluation of the effectiveness of individual group members, the following list of criteria is suggestive:

To what extent do group members attend group meetings regularly and promptly?
Does the group member remain impersonal and direct discussion to group issues rather than personalities?
To what extent do group members participate in group thinking, discussing, planning, deciding, acting, and evaluating?
To what extent is the group member able to think and act in terms of "we" instead of "I"?
To what extent is the group member able to think in a group and express his ideas freely?
To what extent is the group member able to understand the point of view of others and harmonize conflicts as well as accept differences in viewpoints?
To what extent does the group member accept group problems and group goals?
To what extent does the group member make contributions out of his experiences?
To what extent does he do interim work assigned by the group?[36]

The First National Training Laboratory on Group Development held at Bethel, Maine, in July 1947, evaluated growth in group processes in terms of the following:

Intercommunication between members of the group:
   a. Mechanics of communication—vocabulary, rules of procedure, semantic sensitivity, *et cetera*
   b. Permissiveness for all members in expressing fears, needs, concerns, ideas, *et cetera* to the group
Group objectivity toward its own functioning:
   a. Ability by all members to make and accept interpretation about member and group functioning
   b. Ability to collect and use appropriate process—information about itself
Interdependent responsibility by all members for:
   a. Sharing leadership functions—direction setting, being a resource for the group
   b. Achieving skill in flexible adjustment to member and leader when required by the group at various stages of group production

---

[36] Adapted from Trecker, *op. cit.*, p. 101-102.

c. Achieving mutual sensitivity to the needs and styles of participation of the members
   d. Distinguishing between member role contributions and personality characteristics
Group cohesion adequate to permit:
   a. Assimilation of new ideas without group disintegration
   b. Assimilation of new members in a way to strengthen rather than to disrupt the group
   c. Holding to long-range goals
   d. Profiting from success experiences
   e. Learning from failure experiences or realistic goals
   f. Making constructive use of internal conflicts
Group ability to inform itself and to think straight and decide creatively about its problems:
   a. Utilizing contribution potential of all members
   b. Discovering and utilizing appropriate resource materials and persons
   c. Detecting and correcting fallacies in group thinking
Group ability to detect and control rhythms of group metabolism—fatigue, tension, tempo, pace, emotional atmosphere
Satisfactory integrations of member ideologies, needs, and goals with common group traditions, ideology, and goals
Group ability to create new functions and groups as needed and to terminate its existence if and as appropriate.[37]

Criteria of Effective Group Processes

Criteria serve as guides to activity and to identification of the basic operational elements which indicate that democratic group processes are really functioning in a group situation. Many of the criteria of effective group processes which have been formulated and published have been the result of logical analysis and deduction. Starting with basic definitions of group processes the criteria have been deduced from the definitions. Such criteria are often sound, but they have not been put to the test of activity. Perhaps the best statement of operational criteria of group processes is a recent statement by Stephen Corey. While admitting that his principles were based on a deductive approach, Corey, in general, "leaned more heavily upon the inductive approach—inferring principles from practices rather than from definitions.[38]

The essential criteria of group processes formulated by Corey and a summary of his comments on each are:

The goals must be such that group activity will expedite their attainment.
   Group activity cannot meet any and all needs. There is much worthy and educative work that can be done in a highly individualistic manner. Group process, then, is not a panacea, nor is it a pattern into which all

---
[37] National Education Association and Research Center for Group Dynamics, *op. cit.*, Appendix, Sec. III.
[38] Stephen M. Corey, "Principles of Cooperative Group Work," *Group Planning in Education, op. cit.*, p. 130-38.

educational work must be forced. The only justification for group process is that it must lead to greater satisfactions for the group members than any other alternative procedure. Pragmatically, group processes should be used only if they are the most effective processes. Affirmative answers to the following questions imply that it is advisable to use group processes rather than individual planning and action:
1. Is the goal contemplated one sought by all members of the group?
2. Does achievement of the goal by a group as such add to its desirability?
3. Do the means required to achieve the goal use the varied talents of a number of individuals?

Work is undertaken that is relevant to the goals that the group wants to achieve.

Goals are set by the group and the projects undertaken are those that the group believes important, that make "sense" to the members. This does not preclude that a status leader may "suggest" goals; it does mean that such goals are to be treated in the same manner as goals suggested by members of the group. In short, to be effective in motivating group members the goals must be those which the members accept, appreciate, and want to attain. They cannot be "benevolently" imposed from above or the level of cooperation becomes that of exploitation. In group processes, *the participants are facing problems which are vital to them.*

Activities in cooperative group work are in sequence: (a) clarification of goals or purposes, (b) consideration of means for the attainment of these goals, (c) action in terms of the means decided upon, and (d) appraisal or evaluation of consequences.

These steps are Corey's analysis of the group process. It is interesting to note his comment on them: "These phases of cooperative group work as they are named above are apt to imply too much formality. . . . It is easy to go too far insisting, or even suggesting, that any formal series of steps be taken in group work. The all important consideration is to get on with the project at hand and realize its benefits. Any formality should clearly be a means to that end. Pedagogically, the soundest procedure is for the 'steps' to emerge from evaluation of a number of projects. . . . It is obvious, of course, that each of the four steps is not taken seriatim and cleaned up before the next is approached." To summarize, in group processes *the participants are able to do something about the problems they face because there are processes.*

There is free interplay of minds during all stages of the cooperative activity.

A dynamic exchange of experiences pertinent to the problem gives the group the benefit of many points of view. Such discussion is not a debate, nor mere talk; it is relevant to the problem and it moves beyond discussion to action. There are a number of conditions that will increase the probability of this free interplay of minds: (a) all members of the group must be peers as persons; there is no "authority status" to influence free expression through a fear of retribution for expressing candid views; (b) leadership "emerges" from the group—it is not imposed from above; (c) the members of the group must know each other as persons as well as the "professional" talents of each.

A consensus of opinion is striven for.

The group does not decide by a consent majority vote. Rather it moves beyond the "vote" technique, which to many is the essence of democracy, to the establishment of a consensus—an agreement in opinion, or practical unanimity. Group action is never effective when a majority coerces a minority, for the minority in many cases sabotages the work of the group.[39]

To Corey's criteria it seems important to add two others, not with the idea of merely adding more "rules," but rather with the idea of further clarifying this type of activity.

Organization is focused on a problem as the center or base of operation.

In the center, the base must be a problem. A subject or topic is something you talk about. Do-Democracy must go beyond. Problems are things you attempt to solve—to do something about. The group thinks, discusses, plans, decides, acts, and evaluates in terms of a specific problem. With the problem in the center of the group process, the special abilities that reside in all members of the group are most likely to be tapped.

We know a number of things about the effectiveness of the problem-centered group. The small group is not only the most effective, but it affords the greatest opportunity for effective action in all six phases of group process, consensus, intensity of face-to-face contacts, maximum individual participation, and those vital attachments which are created only in the intimacy of close association. The *organization* must also give promise of (a) being functional; (b) facilitating widespread participation and good human relationships; (c) fulfilling a constructive social purpose that the group accepts; and (d) providing for a continuity of problem-solving.

The factor of heterogeneity is utilized.

In addition, problem-centered groups invite the help of all; they are not homogeneous, but heterogeneous. In a group containing too few differences there is little stimulus to changing behavior. An effective problem-centered group takes advantage of the number of diversified abilities and needs and integrates them into an organized, unified endeavor. It aims at achieving unity in general purpose, and diversity in ways of achieving that purpose. We must learn to value conflicts arising out of diversities as the starting point in change and to develop them into a new synthesis.

Group Leadership

Effective group leadership is crucial to the success of group processes. In spite of the fact that they express belief in the democratic way of life,

---
[39] Corey, *op. cit.*, p. 130-38.

many people are confused about the role of leadership in democratic group processes and have no clear values to use as guides when they are selecting leaders or when they are themselves in a leadership role. The leader in group processes is above all a guide in democratic group experiencing, not a dictator of the thinking and acting of group members. Traditionally, the leader has been conceived as someone *above* the group, and not *in* the group. Even in our democratic society this idea of leadership has been adhered to in industry, business, and education.

In the experiments of Lippitt and those of Bavelas previously mentioned, the problems of leadership plays an important role. Lippitt's experiment with the effects of democratic and autocratic group atmosphere indicated that a group atmosphere can be changed in a relatively short time from autocratic to democratic and vice versa by introducing new leadership techniques. Bavelas' work in leadership training substantiates Lippitt's findings. These studies give us some clues about democratic leadership.

The Leadership Role

Both autocratic and democratic leadership consists of playing a certain role. The leadership role cannot be performed without followers who play complementary roles, either as democratic or autocratic followers. The difference between authoritarian and democratic leadership does not lie in the amount of power the leader possesses, but in the function and position the leader has in the group. In an authoritarian atmosphere the leader is not a member of the group. Often he is a member of a "higher" class set *over* the group without the group's wishes. Such a leader is not accountable to the group for his actions, but only to those above; he allows the group to know only what he feels is good for them, and he keeps the power of decision and formation of policy in his own hands. This leadership role is leadership by the "elite." The authoritarian leader feels that the majority are born to be followers, that only a few are "gifted" with leadership. In short, he is *over* the group, not *of* the group

In democratic group processes, leadership *is not a function of position*. Leadership emerges from the group. The leader is *of* the group, is selected by the group, is responsible to the group for his actions. He remains in power by group support; he is only one element in group processes—a guiding element. Leadership and intelligent followership reside in each individual and the success or failure of the group purposes will be determined by how well each person performs these functions.

In group processes leaders are moved into their leadership roles through the efforts of the group to achieve the group goals while utilizing the most competent leadership of group intelligence as it emerges from the group. A group leader does not *begin* with authority, he *ends* with it. Authority, then, is never a function of position, but it resides in the group and is delegated as responsibilities of various kinds fall on different shoulders. In effective group processes there is no Führer, no "leader."

Howard Lane gives an apt description of this emerging leadership role, "In a group presuming to be democratic, or to train for living in a democracy, the conception of discipline (control) becomes one of leadership (the release and coordination of human potentialities). Accepted leadership is essential to the effective exercise of group intelligence. It derives its position and influence from the respect of the group for its peculiar competencies rather than from ordained status."[40]

In group processes, then, everyone should have opportunities to lead and to follow. Democratic group processes utilize for group benefit the intelligence and contributions of all. This means very simply that leadership moves from person to person. Democratic group processes are not functioning if abilities within the group are so divergent and interest so individual that the relationship between individuals remains frozen, with the same few always leading and the many following.

Indeed, changing roles is one of the difficult aspects of group processes. Studies of personality have revealed that a person's attitude toward his role in group processes is often a cause of maladjustment. If an individual were accustomed to the security of cooperating dependently, and then were placed in a group situation where he must play the role of a leader, or if he were accustomed to lead, and now had to follow; changes in role from leader to follower or vice versa are difficult.

Effective group processes demand that one be able to be both intelligent in leadership and followership. These roles are constantly interchanging and interacting. One must be capable of alternately leading and following. Lewin points out that establishing democratic group processes requires active education, "The democratic follower has to learn to play a role which implies, among other points, a fair share of responsibility toward the group and a sensitivity to other people's feelings. . . . What holds for the education of democratic followers also holds true for the education of democratic leaders. In fact, it seems to be the same process through which persons learn to play either of these roles and it seems that both roles have to be learned if either one is to be played well."[41]

---

[40] Lane, *op. cit.*, p. 4-5
[41] Lewin, "Dynamics of Group Action," *op. cit.*, p. 199.

Types of Group Leadership

In democratic group processes two leadership roles are possible: (a) the role of the "guiding" or "status" leader, such as a teacher, supervisor, chairman, board president and (b) the role of "shared" or "emerging" leadership. The status leader is one placed in a "leadership" position because of special preparation and competence; he aids the group in discovering worthy goals and in establishing good group procedures, but does not always remain the leader. Shared leadership emerges from the group itself in group efforts to get concerted action toward group goals. These cannot be considered separate and distinct types of leadership since shared leadership is constantly emerging in a group having a status leader.

Kilpatrick has clearly described shared leadership:

> "Many seem to think of leadership as if it were only or primarily fixed in advance, either by appointment or election or by special ability and preparation. On this basis, they proceed to divide people into two fixed groups, leaders and followers. Such a view seems inadequate, quite denied by observable facts. Actual leadership as we see it comes mostly by emergence out of a social situation. A number of people talk freely about a matter of common concern. *A* proposes a plan of action. *B* successfully voices objection and criticism. *C* then proposes a modified plan. *D, E,* and *F* criticize certain features of this plan. The group at this point divides, seemingly unable to agree. *G* then comes forward with a new plan that combines the desired features and avoids the evils feared. The group agrees. Here *A, B, C, D, E, F,* and *G* were successively leaders of the group. And each such act of leadership emerged out of the situation as it then appeared. This is democratic leadership and its success depends on—nay exactly is—an on-going process of education inherent in the situation."[42]

Status leadership has been too often autocratic, but it need not be. In circumstances where leadership is derived from institutionalized authority, as in the case of teachers, administrators, and supervisors in a school, status leaders need not act like Führers. As Lane [43] points out the group under status leadership will become intelligent only if it accepts as reasonable the limits of its freedom of choice and action. Group processes do not function democratically when they become an exercise in guessing what the status leader has in mind or will accept. A status leader must offer freedom of choice, and once he has done so he may not use veto power.

Responsibilities and Functions of Leadership

Whether the leader emerges from the group or is a status leader makes little difference with regard to functions and responsibilities. However,

---

[42] William H. Kilpatrick in Samuel Everett (ed.), *The Community School.* New York: D. Appleton Century, 1940. p. 20.
[43] Lane, *op. cit.,* p. 5.

in order to clarify the thinking of many in the field of education who are status leaders it might help to consider briefly the responsibilities and functions of a status leader in a group. Leadership which is status in nature is primarily a helping process; it is an effort to provide leadership of a continuously helpful kind to all group members so that each may advance the group to more significant service and accomplishment. Status leadership helps groups and group members to:

—discover group goals sufficiently vital so that they will call forth a maximum of cooperative effort.
—set up a system of values enabling the group to define, select, or choose the needs and interests of first priority.
—instill in others a desire to "belong" and to take active part in group action.
—discover their skills, competencies, interests, and abilities so that each, while taking part in group processes, may gain the maximum security which results from each having a part to play and a contribution to make.
—develop good human relationships and satisfactory personal interactions so that a cooperative, permissive atmosphere characterizes group functioning.

Miel has clearly stated the functions of a status leader somewhat as follows: (a) improving human relations within the group; (b) furnishing expertness along certain lines; (c) generating leadership in others; (d) coordinating the efforts of others.[44]

In order to be an effective group leader a status leader must help set the emotional tone in the group. He understands and appreciates people and, what is most important, he has respect for the unique contributions which each group member can make under free, confident, permissive, psychological conditions. A good status leader can help people to get along with one another and develop satisfactory, interpersonal relationships. In short, he is a principal "climate-making" factor in the group. Group processes are interacting processes—processes of interaction between the leaders and followers, the efficiency of which often depends on the "climate" in the group. By his behavior the leader must foster confidence, ease, security, and poise in others so they will be willing to contribute.

Cooperative action is basic to group processes. A skilled status leader can help others to learn to think, discuss, plan, decide, act, and evaluate together. Although a status leader need not be an expert in some academic field, he should be skilled in the techniques of group action. One of his prime responsibilities is to help the group function as a group, to

---
[44] Miel, *op. cit.*, p. 159-62.

help it learn the techniques of group action. However, the technical skills of group action which the leader may possess are not a substitute for behaving democratically. To be effective the leader's behavior must typify the cooperative behavior essential on the part of all group members. If the leader expects the group to behave democratically, he must be *of* the group, and not *over* it. Not only must he talk democratically, he must *do* democratically.

Another significant function of leadership is the discovering and releasing of further leadership within the group. Within each group there is a wealth of leadership if only it is called forth. Leadership in the most efficient group processes springs from the individual competencies and resources of the group itself. To tap these potentialities is the task of any effective leader. More and more people must be given the opportunities to share in leadership responsibilities, and leadership must be entrusted to the person best qualified at any given time to guide the group toward its goals.

Coordinating the efforts of others is basic to effective group processes. The leader is in a position where he can see the total situation; hence he can help the group move toward consensus as to goals and paths of action, the evaluation of resources needed to attain the goals, the planning of ends-means procedures, the making of decisions, and the delegation and acceptance of responsibilities by various group members for action. Pulling together the various competencies in a group so that they result in concerted action necessitates effective coordination and a balance between gradualism and rapidity of change in moving forward.

To be an effective coordinator the group leader starts where the group is. He respects the need of the group for security in processes and helps the group move away from status quo securities. He avoids short-cutting the group processes in order to make them more "efficient." Fiats, standardization of processes, power tactics, key personnel may get things done in a hurry, but not democratically. An effective group leader never gives the "answers" to a problem. Too often group members ask the leader for "answers"—immediate, specific solutions for the group problems. The group leader can best serve by coordinating the efforts of the group in finding its own answers.

Leadership, which is shared or which emerges from the group situation, serves the same functions just described as being the prime responsibilities of a status leader. Democratic group leadership has a possessive belief in democracy and demonstrates this belief in behavior; it has a belief in group processes, the emergence of group thinking, discussing, planning, deciding, acting, and evaluating, as of greater value in achieving group goals in a democracy than the separate act of any single group member. It possesses skills in the techniques of group processes resulting from living in and participating with a group; it shapes conditions within a group so that democratic interrelationships are established and guides the group members to an ever-increasing level of maturity in intelligent leadership and followership.

Leadership is not a specific attribute of personality which some persons possess and others do not. Leaders cannot be entirely distinguished from followers, for the same person may be a leader at one time and a follower at another. The words "leader" and "follower" are thus more accurately applied to the roles that are played in group processes than to personality types. Leadership becomes then a function of the situation in which it is observed. When a group faces a problem, leadership will emerge in accordance with the needs of the group. When the needs of the group are met by the competencies of one leader, he is no longer a leader and leadership passes to another.

A true leader must be accepted as a member of the group, for leader and followers are interdependent. Each needs the other, and the accomplishment of common group goals requires that both types of roles be filled by members of the group. Leaders in one situation should not hesitate to be followers in another situation demanding competencies and skills possessed in a greater degree by another group member. Indeed, only ego-goals, which one considers more important than group goals, can cause an effective group member to refuse the role of follower for fear of losing status in the group. Followers, as well as leaders, share in achieving group goals and both contribute in the process.

To summarize, in group processes leader and followers have shared group goals. They are moving jointly toward these goals. The leader is a group member, chosen because he has special competencies to help the group obtain goals desired by both leader and followers. His authority is something he *ends* with, rather than *begins* with; it is authority *along with,* rather than *over* the group members. The leader's main function is a helping function, the direction of the activities of the group in more effective processes. Effective group leadership implies helping the member to select the ends-means procedures necessary for attaining group goals. A true leader neither needs nor uses machinery to maintain his status; he relinquishes the position of leadership when his particular competencies are no longer needed. He is aware of his dependence upon his followers as well as their dependence on his contributions, and the relationship between leader and follower is charcterized by democratic interaction which liberates the best that each has to contribute toward the solution of a common problem.

Leadership Preparation—a Statement of Position

Research in the field of leadership training has contributed very little positive information. For the most part available data indicates quite clearly that leadership is not a personality trait and that leaders can be trained. Zeleny's work in leadership training indicates that individuals can be trained in effective group leadership, "All experimental evidence . . . indicates that leadership ability can be developed by instruction and practice in leadership. . . . If leaders (or followers) are to be developed for participation in civic groups, the practice must be done in groups of a character similar to real life groups; only in this way can the effort expended in instruction show good returns in terms of practical performance." [45]

Bavelas in his study of small group leadership found that training for democratic leadership demanded training by democratic means as well as the presence of a democratic atmosphere and behavior on the part of the trainer.[46] It is important to understand that democratic group leadership cannot be learned by autocratic methods. Effective group leadership can be learned only by participating in a democratic group. No talk about democratic leadership can be a substitute for democratic doing. The best preparation possible for group leadership is participation in group processes on an ever-increasing level of maturity; indeed, effective group processes are leadership training for every participant. Democratic leadership emerges through practice in being an effective group member. In short, instruction in group leadership, which is not integrated with actual practice in group participation, is no guarantee that the leadership will be either effective or democratic.

By Way of Conclusion

Using group processes is not just another passing fad. In this highly complex world of ours many minds are needed to solve successfully and democratically problems which are the concern of all. Efficiency in working together democratically and getting something done is the over-all goal of group processes. As such it is an effective learning process if we conceive all behavior as goal seeking. Group processes result in a change in group behavior as well as a change in individual behavior. Learning

---

[45] Leslie Zeleny, "Experiments in Leadership Training," *Journal of Educational Sociology*, XVI, January 1941. p. 312-13.
[46] Bavelas, *op. cit.*, p. 143-65.

is, in its simplest analysis, the result of the progressive changes which a group makes in the logic of its experiences due to its increasingly purposeful efforts to resolve its problems by developing better ends-means procedures in progressing toward group goals. The use of group processes results in learning the understandings, skills, and attitudes which characterize them. This includes all of the phases of group processes—group thinking, discussing, planning, deciding, acting, and evaluating.

Group processes are a valuable learning situation for both the leader and participants for: (a) the best preparation for democratic living is group experiencing by means of participation in democratic group processes; (b) everyone is in on it and complete member potential is brought to bear on a problem; (c) it is an effective method of social action—of moving from one problem to another with the cooperative action of all involved in making the decision; (d) it develops better and more satisfying human relationships.

Indeed, the very fate of the democratic ideal in these days of uncertainty may well rest on the ability of democratic groups to develop effective processes—ways of doing things—which will exemplify democratic behavior in progressing toward desired goals.

Group Processes in Action

How well do supervisors use democratic group processes?
Must the steps in group processes be used in sequence to be effective?
Must the group be aware at all times that they are using the processes; that is, must the process "always show"?
Are democratic group processes applicable to all kinds of situations in which supervisors function?
How do the processes work in curriculum building, in putting the curriculum into operation, in child study, in determining the kinds of school buildings to erect, in selecting and developing evaluation instruments, and in introducing new teacher procedures?
Are group processes equally effective in working with teachers, with administrators, and with the community?

All these and other questions this chapter attempts to answer by describing a number of situations where group processes were used by supervisors *on the job* with teachers, administrators, and community leaders. Each story describes the operation of the processes in a particular situation, some of which are rural, some city; in some, elementary teachers are involved, in others, secondary; while still others involve both; in some, one supervisor is the status leader, in others, several supervisors work together as group leaders. In a few instances the stories are unfinished because at the time the situation was described the process was still in operation and the "action" step was incomplete. In each instance, the writer has attempted to describe the situation, identify the problem, describe what was done, and point out the role which the supervisor played as a status leader and/or a change-agent in the process.

Identifying the Problems of Teachers

It was the expressed desire of a number of teachers responsible for the activities of the rural teachers' clubs in San Diego County, California, that they might meet with others who had like responsibilities in the other clubs to discuss problems and to share ideas. The elementary coordinators serving these rural teachers' clubs capitalized upon this idea and suggested that the county superintendent call a planning meeting for representatives of the clubs. Although a number of the clubs had been in existence for a long period of time, this was the first time an attempt was made to consider the problems of rural teachers' clubs on a county-wide basis. Since there was a definite trend toward making the teachers' club programs an integral part of the county program for in-service professional growth of teachers, the members of the county staff felt that there was a definite need for greater unity of effort in the club activities.

County-Wide Planning Is a First Step

The meeting was planned, and its purposes were discussed with the presidents of the seven rural teachers' clubs. They were all interested and anxious to participate in this cooperative planning endeavor. Each president chose two members of his club planning committee to represent the group at the county-wide meeting. A personal invitation was then issued to each representative by the county superintendent.

The meeting began with a luncheon served by members of the county staff. Seating was arranged in such a way that everyone had an opportunity to become acquainted with representatives from other areas. This period of informal conversation tended to break down the reserve often felt in groups composed of relative strangers. Seated at the tables were the two representatives from each teachers' club, the three elementary coordinators, the music coordinator, one of the guidance-attendance coordinators who serve the rural schools, the county superintendent, the director of curriculum, and the assistant superintendent responsible for special services.

Following the luncheon, the group adjourned to a comfortable conference room where the county superintendent initiated the discussion. In a brief presentation he emphasized the importance of the rural teachers' clubs in the total county program of education and the relationship of the clubs to county, state, and national teachers' organizations. As guides to the thinking of the group he presented the following problems as being of major importance to the deliberations of the afternoon:

1. Determining how the teachers' clubs could better meet the needs of rural teachers
2. Finding ways by which the county office could serve the clubs in helping to effect a program to meet these needs.

Varied Suggestions Come Forth

Following the leader's able identification of the problems confronting the group, the participants shared their experiences and ideas. Subsidiary problems were raised and possible solutions suggested. The need for long-term planning and for planning committees to function throughout the year received major emphasis in the discussion. The representatives also felt that the elementary coordinator in each area should act as a consultant to the planning committees in her area. Many felt a need for the clubs to sponsor small group meetings in addition to their regular monthly meetings in order to meet the varied needs and interests of the members. Some expressed the feeling that their clubs should have a regular meeting time and that a theme for the annual club program would provide greater continuity for their activities. All felt that their meeting should provide time for professional development, business, a report from the coordinator, and social activity. The possibility of having joint meetings of clubs with similar interests was discussed, and many different types of professional activities were suggested for the club programs.

Before the meeting was concluded, the leader summarized the suggestions which had been offered and pointed up their relationship to the major problems which had been identified at the beginning of the discussion. A summary statement of the discussion and conclusions was later sent to all who had attended the meeting and to the teachers' club presidents to assist them when they met with their respective planning committees.

A Small Group Identifies Problems

As an example, the planning meeting of one of the teachers' clubs might be described. The planning committee of this club was composed of the incoming president who had been one of the representatives at the county-wide meeting, the other representative, and three other teachers who were interested in the program for the ensuing year. The elementary coordinator was asked to sit with the group as a consultant. The president acted as the discussion leader.

The initial discussion included a report of the county-wide meeting by the leader and general suggestions from the group. It was soon evident that there were three problems involved. This committee had first to determine the problems on which the club wished to work during the year, then the type of meetings best suited to the total group of twenty-five teachers who comprised the membership of the club, and finally the schedule of meetings.

Discussion regarding these three problems followed. The leader organized and summarized the suggestions, including those from the county-wide meeting which were relevant to the specific situation. From this, the committee decided upon a theme or problem to be studied and organized a program for the next year, including dates for meetings, topics, speakers, and leaders.

It was the consensus of the various planning committees that the county-wide discussion meeting had been of invaluable service in helping them to identify their problems and develop more vital professional programs for the rural teachers' clubs. A general request for a similar meeting the following year resulted.

Developing School Goals

As plans for the 1945-46 school year of the San Dieguito Union High School in San Diego County, California, were discussed by the district superintendent with members of his school board, the teaching staff, and the county superintendent of schools and staff members, it became evident that among the problems to be dealt with were the following:

1. Since over seventy percent of the school graduates were not entering institutions of higher learning, the prevailing curriculum emphasis on college preparation was in need of re-examination.

2. Withdrawal from the school before graduation by twenty-one percent of those entering the seventh grade indicated the necessity of a study to determine how the curriculum might better serve these adolescents and how they might be kept in school for a longer period.

3. The giving of 102 failing marks and almost 400 "incompletes" in June 1945 revealed a need for an analysis of reasons for such failure and frustration.

4. Changes in the community resulting from the war pointed to the need of a community survey on which an improved curriculum could be based.

5. Very large teacher-turnover for the ensuing year necessitated the development by the group of a harmonious philosophy of education and agreement on school objectives.

A Workshop for Problem Solution

In order to develop school goals and to cope with the curriculum problems of the San Dieguito Union High School, it was cooperatively decided by the school administration, teachers, and county school representatives that a three-week summer workshop should be planned and conducted just prior to the opening of school in September 1945. Interest of the teaching staff in the proposal was so strong that 100 percent of them volunteered to participate in the workshop without any additional salary. The board of trustees for the school district encouraged the project by authorizing the expenditure of money to employ a curriculum consultant from one of the major universities of the state to serve as director of the workshop. In addition, the board expressed its willingness to accept teacher participation in the workshop in lieu of summer session work at a university for "salary hurdle credit." County school office interest in the project was evidenced by the provision of numerous educational services.

The Schedule for Group Work

The workshop group met as a whole body for the first four days and then from 8 A.M. to 10 A.M. daily. After a recess, members of the group reconvened for the remainder of the morning and in the afternoon for committee work. Recreation and entertainment were planned as afternoon and evening events. Lines of approach to developing school goals in the workshop were these:

1. The first morning was devoted to an analysis and discussion of recent sociological changes which held implications for the school program. This session was designed to challenge the teachers to dare to do things in new ways if critical analysis warranted new procedures.

2. A brief review of the Educational Policies Commission's *Planning for All American Youth*[1] as one way the school might organize to meet changed social conditions followed on the second morning.

3. On the third day of the workshop, the implications of the local community's current social scene in the light of its peculiar needs and characteristics were discussed. The secretary of the local chamber of commerce and three members of the high school board of trustees were present and contributed information concerning the community and school.

The nature of the community was considered along these broad lines: (a) the history of its founding, growth, and development; (b) the nature of the population as to distribution, racial composition, mobility, births and deaths, occupations, income range, bank deposits, savings, living standards, housing and land tenure, and political-social-cultural aspects; (c) commercial activities; (d) public services; and (e) possibilities for growth and development along various lines.

This data included the available types of occupational employment in the area, the agricultural conditions, the percentage of high school graduates going to college, the percentage of drop-outs before graduation, the percentage of failures and where the greatest failures were, financial and tax information, the daily schedule, and brief statements from each teacher of the work going on in each course taught. Bibliographical materials were also made available to the group.

On this third day, workshoppers divided themselves into five committees to consider the following aspects of the school goals: common learnings, guidance, health and physical fitness, special and vocational interests. Specific spearhead questions were formulated by the consultant designed to bring out the implications for the teachers themselves.

4. On the fourth day, the problem and techniques of surveying the local school and community resources were considered.

5. Then, for several days, the committees met, returning finally to the total group, in each case with a report to be evaluated by the total group.

---
[1] National Education Association, Washington, D. C., 1945.

Leadership in Providing Resources

Preceding the workshop there had been a marshalling of available resources by the curriculum coordinator; bibliographies had been prepared and duplicated; and reference books and pamphlets had been assembled from the county school library, the county school curriculum laboratory, and from the school professional library. Many samples of courses of study and resource units had been secured from widely scattered parts of the United States. New professional books had been added to these resources previous to the opening of the workshop. Arrangements had also been made with selected professional and lay persons to participate in designated sessions of the workshop.

Attention on Continuous Leadership Development

The matter of coordinating the varied activities of workshop members in their work as a total group or in committees became a matter of great concern to the curriculum coordinator very early in the workshop period. The matter of group dynamics was involved. The curriculum coordinator, considering himself a fellow-laborer with his colleagues rather than the "outside" expert, approached his task with an experimental point of view. He perceived that certain characteristics are desirable in group leadership. For example, first, it must be distributed responsibility; second, it is an act of faith in the democratic process; third, it must open the way for democratic action; and fourth, it must be based on profound optimism as to the capacity of human beings to grow and change for the better.

Furthermore, the coordinator recognized that stimulation of the teachers by various means in the development of their own plans for improvement should be the broad objective in curriculum development. These three criteria were used to determine whether group action in setting up school goals should be fostered:

Is the goal contemplated one sought by all members of the group?
Does achievement of the goal by a group as such add to its desirability?
Do the means required to achieve the goal use the varied talents of a number of individuals?[2]

Other principles of cooperative group work have emerged as the San Dieguito staff has continued to work: (a) activities of the group have been relevant in increasing degree to the goals being striven for; (b)

---

[2] Stephen M. Corey, *Group Planning in Education*, 1945 Yearbook. National Education Association, Department of Supervision and Curriculum Development. Washington: The Department, 1945. p. 131.

these activities, more and more, tend to follow a sequential pattern of clarification of goals, consideration of means of attainment followed by appropriate action, and evaluation; (c) free interaction among group members is a constant; and (d) a group decision is sought.

Following the workshop activity, the curriculum coordinator, insofar as determination of school objectives are concerned, has sought to develop self-sustaining power in the individuals and groups with whom he has worked. Several things have been done from time to time in this respect.

1. He has constantly urged group chairmen to give much time to pre-planning their meetings. This has necessitated securing the cooperation of the superintendent in adjustment of teacher load, daily schedule, and provision for additional resource materials. He has endeavored to sit with these pre-planning groups as a fellow-worker.

2. He has from time to time presented to the group questions designed to bring about re-evaluation of the statement of school goals.

3. He has introduced resource persons to specific groups—specialists in health, music, science, and other areas.

4. He has fostered rotating chairmanships on the curriculum committees.

5. He has encouraged recording of all important proceedings through the use of secretaries and recording machines.

6. He has suggested that a critical observer be appointed for each major meeting. This advice has not as yet been followed.

7. He has arranged for summer session workshop opportunities at neighboring institutions of higher learning for some of the faculty members so that they could examine their formulations of objectives from a new angle.

8. He has continuously striven to convince the school administration of the advisability of providing adequate time, space, and materials for the efficient carrying on of the curriculum project, particularly to make possible such community-faculty-pupil interaction as will result in a constant re-evaluation of goals and means of reaching them. There has been partial success in this respect.

9. He has secured some degree of teacher-pupil cooperation in the study of pupil and community needs as a basis for setting up goals, particularly in the fields of health and vocational education.

10. He has helped make available several basic studies and analyses of the social scene and curriculum development.

Determining Curriculum Content

The science curriculum needed changing. It had been fifteen years since the program in the junior high schools had been revised, and the recently developed course of study for the tenth grade had never been accepted or followed by the teachers. Each teacher rode his own hobby and taught what he pleased with consequent overlapping and repetition, particularly in the ninth-grade elective course and the tenth-grade required course.

Everyone recognized the need but was afraid to move since previous meetings between the science teachers of the junior and senior high schools had always resulted in a stalemate as each group supported its program and refused to listen to the other. The problem was accentuated because there had been no over-all curriculum planning. The junior high school supervisor worked independently of the senior high school department, and both had developed intrenched interests which they defended at all costs.

Emphasis Placed on Over-All Planning

The new curriculum director had sensed this problem when he came into the system and had suggested that the supervisors hold regular staff meetings to discuss problems affecting both the elementary and secondary segments so that an over-all curriculum framework could be developed and the same philosophy operate from kindergarten through the junior college. This central committee had been operating for a year and a half before the curriculum director thought the time was ripe for tackling the science program.

Through the offices of the junior and senior high school supervisors, a committee of science teachers was appointed, each member of the committee representing the science teachers in a specific school. At the first meeting the curriculum director assumed the leadership, introduced the problem, and saw to it that each person on the committee had a chance to present the problem as seen by the teachers in his building. It was the last time that the curriculum director had that privilege. From then on the teachers took over the leadership, elected their chairman, developed their plans, and assumed responsibility for the committee's work. The supervisors and the curriculum director continued as members of the committee, and a junior high school principal, elected by the principals' club, also became a committee member.

Problems Need Joint Solution

At that first meeting when the problem was analyzed, numerous sub-problems were presented: the eight-grade program was too crowded and too difficult; some teachers became so interested in a unit that all the time was given to it and the pupils did not get a balanced program; the pupils from some junior high schools found the tenth-grade program an exact duplication of their ninth-grade course; the omission of biology from the tenth grade meant that some pupils with a strong science interest could not get biology if they took chemistry and physics in their junior and senior years; the present science requirement threw students without science interest or aptitude into laboratory science courses for which they were wholly unsuited. And so it went. The problems were numerous but, to the surprise of the supervisors, the teachers from the junior high school agreed with those from the senior high school that neither group could solve them alone.

One meeting of all the science teachers, at which the teacher-elected chairman presided, laid the problem with all its ramifications before the total group. Again there was consensus that the program must be revised and a planned scope and sequence developed. There was great difference of opinion, however, as to what should be done. Subcommittees were set up, and each junior and senior high school group discussed the problems in its department meeting. These reports were brought back to the city-wide committee by the building representative where they were threshed out, harmonized, revised, and referred back to the school groups for suggestions and approval.

Before the end of the school year, the Science Committee had arrived at a program on which all the science teachers could agree and which solved most of the problems which had caused conflict for so long between the two divisions. The program still had to have the approval of both the Junior High School and the Senior High School Committees on the Curriculum and of the General Committee on the Curriculum. Here, again, the teachers took the lead and the chairman presented the program so successfully that it won the approval of all three.

Action Follows Solution

But the work of the committee had not ended. Resource units had to be developed, so the committee continued its meetings throughout the following school year. Subcommittees were appointed to work on units, gather materials, preview audio-visual sources, and try out the activities and projects as they were developed. As the units took form they were reviewed by the Science Committee which acted as a coordinating and steering committee. Throughout this whole development the curriculum director and the supervisors acted as consultants, helped with the planning, marshalled the resources of their offices, saw that mimeographed materials were ready when needed, and encouraged lagging spirits when the going got rough. By the end of the second year, the units for the two-year Practical Science course had progressed so far that a small committee was appointed to work in the summer curriculum workshop editing them and putting them into form for publication.

The Developing Program Belonged to All

While this procedure has many defects, it also has features which recommend it and which work well for a large city system. Most important of all, group processes had been used and many people had participated in them. Teacher behavior had been modified as a result of the sharing of experience among fellow teachers; leadership had developed; and, through the appointment of many subcommittees, numerous teachers had had an opportunity to lead and contribute to the development of the program. The status leaders, while assuming leadership at the beginning, had surrendered their role early in the process but had remained throughout as members of the group, serving as consultants and giving encouragement as needed. By drawing all the teachers into the process, consensus had been reached and everyone had a stake in the new program. Each felt that it was "their" program and not one that had been handed down from above or one developed by a single teacher and given to them to follow. Group morale had improved as each felt that his contributions had been appreciated and had contributed to improving the science program of the city and to the learning situation for pupils.

Putting the Curriculum into Operation

A Teachers' Curriculum Commission has been the major center of curriculum study for many years in the school system of Burbank, California. Being an outgrowth of the local teachers' association, it has been definitely a teacher organization. Much study, the production of some materials, and recommendations for curriculum changes and additions have been accomplished.

With the introduction of workshops, the tie-up with the actual daily experiences of children has been more effective. These have been sponsored by the Teachers' Curriculum Commission and have been of major importance in the in-service growth of large groups of teachers. Study of curriculum problems continues and materials are produced, but each is more definitely related to specific classroom activities. In addition, there is much teacher experimentation with the media which children use, observation of fellow teachers and children in the curriculum in action, and immediate evaluation of the effectiveness of these experiences. Since interrelationships of individuals and groups are based on more *doing,* and not so predominantly on *discussion,* excellent human relationships have also developed.

In organizing workshops each fall, the Teachers' Curriculum Commission sends out a questionnaire to all teachers, both old and new, with a few suggestions as to workshops previously requested and an opportunity for additional requests. Based on frequency of request, a workable number of groups is then established with a teacher chairman and secretary and a qualified supervisor as leader.

Because of their very practical value, all workshops have been given a high evaluation by teachers. Professional growth credit has been requested and granted to teachers for these workshops. One unit of credit comparable to university credit is given for the usual ten and a half hours of meeting and fifteen hours of outside work. During the past two years workshops have been held in art, music, audio-visual education, guidance, reading, skill subjects, block activity, and kindergarten curriculum.

Kindergarten Teachers Join Forces

The kindergarten workshop, with its purposes, problems, organization, and outcomes, is described here as an example of the workshop technique for putting the curriculum into operation. Developed in the spring of 1945, at the enthusiastic request of thirty-five kindergarten teachers, it included almost 100 percent of that teaching group. These teachers had tried earnestly, yet found a scarcity of stimulating resources on kindergarten problems available in educational literature or university offerings.

A questionnaire, with requests for specific kindergarten problems needing attention, became the basis for planning. A small steering committee of teachers and the supervisor compiled these problems and prepared possible ways of working for the consideration of the entire group at its first workshop meeting. Since recent growth in enrollment has brought teachers from many areas out of the state, with certain variations in training and experience, this discussion was quite challenging. After considerable discussion and some constructive adjustments, long-time plans were agreed upon by the group.

Two major desires of the entire teacher group were (a) to observe and evaluate together as much kindergarten curriculum *in action* as possible, within the classroom or through demonstration; and (b) to study together selected problems, preparing or revising related bulletins and other materials. Since all kindergartens had afternoon sessions, it was usually possible, through the cooperation of principals, to excuse teachers for short periods of observation. On other occasions teachers observed in two sections—one being released and the alternate teacher not going to the workshop until her class was dismissed. It was further decided by the group to meet each week in a different kindergarten room and to spend approximately half of each meeting in first-hand observations of pupil activities and in the manipulation of essential media. The second half was to be devoted to individual committee study of the other selected problems.

Needs Are Identified and Work Shared

Committee study, based on six needs expressed by the group, included:

A review of the kindergarten curriculum as a basis for constructing a teachers' guide another year

Preparation of an illustrated booklet on the kindergarten to supplement parent understanding gained through observation and study groups

Re-evaluation of teacher-parent conference plan and revision of child's record sheet

Preparation of basic list of kindergarten books for children, teachers, and parents

Preparation of standard list of supplies and equipment

Preparation of record sheet, which would help teacher understand these children, as a basis for first-grade experiences.

Teachers chose the committee which they most desired. Chairmen and secretaries were elected in each group, specific objectives decided upon, and ways of working and individual responsibilities planned. Since each member was eager to know what the other committees were doing, and since many times an individual was capable of making worth-while contributions to several committees, the group discussed ways of sharing. It was decided that committee progress reports should be made to the entire group from time to time, permitting evaluation and contribution by all. This plan proved a very effective means of personal and group interrelationship.

Research Goes on in Working Situations

Classroom observations of group members and their children in action as a basis for the study of best curriculum practices were carried out in an excellent manner. Music, clay, finger painting, block activity, and the rest period were demonstrated at separate meetings. Science activities were skillfully portrayed by one member through an excellent display and discussion of materials and equipment. A clever dramatization by other group members of both desirable and undesirable parent conference techniques was one highlight of the workshop. Throughout all of the workshop meetings there was constant emphasis on the importance of understanding the growth characteristics of children and on adequate classroom environment.

The supervisor-leader served as a group member and resource adviser during the entire workshop series. At no time did she give a major talk or conduct a specific demonstration. Her responsibilities in general included:

> Helping establish a friendly, secure, "we work together" feeling;
> Helping encourage shy teachers and "slow down" over-aggressive ones;
> Helping teachers plan specific demonstrations, helping chairmen of separate committees, helping secretaries with more effective minutes;
> Helping chairmen steer discussions in constructive directions;
> Helping supply bibliography and point the direction toward out-of-town recourses;
> Helping with necessary administrative details.

Evaluation Identifies Accomplishment

General evaluation of the workshop was a cooperative enterprise at the last meeting. Teachers were surprised at the vast amount which had been accomplished and heartily voted the experiences as most valuable. Evaluation sheets, with evaluation of the entire workshop and suggestions for future emphasis, were handed in to the chairman. A report of the fifteen hours of outside work as related to various committees and other responsibilities was also compiled.

In summarizing teachers' evaluations, the following points predominated:

> The entire series provided a very "happy" and valuable experience.
> Many practical suggestions for techniques and organization were derived from each aspect emphasized.
> They were glad they all had a chance to take part—the "shy" ones made this comment, particularly.
> They learned that a great deal could be accomplished through cooperative effort.
> All agreed that too much was attempted or that the series should have lasted longer.

From the supervisor's point of view the growth of teachers during this experience was outstanding. It was interesting to note emphasis in science and clay appearing in rooms immediately following its emphasis in the workshop. It was also most evident that the teachers, who thought their way was right, became much more open-minded.

All of the specific objectives set up were accomplished except the completion of the parent booklet and the teacher's guide. Since these are long-time projects, they will be worked on another year. The most important accomplishment undoubtedly was the active, enthusiastic, democratic participation by each one of the thirty-five workshop members.

Developing Social Sensitivity in a Faculty Group

It was the first teachers' meeting of the year and the supervisor and principal were sitting with the thirteen teachers of an elementary school. The school has classes from kindergarten through the eighth grade and is located in a rapidly growing town whose prosperity is almost entirely dependent upon farming activities in the surrounding countryside. The school is housed in a building built in 1913. The school population has grown rapidly, and although three new units have just been completed, two grades still meet in the school auditorium and two in the basement. Three of the teachers are working on emergency credentials. Anglo-, Mexican, and Negro-American children comprise the school population. About one-fourth of the children are of minority group background. Many of the children are from low-income groups, and in the fall of the year the children of migrant workers are registered.

After some introductory remarks, which included expressions of pleasure because of the new rooms and some optimistic words regarding the promise of the general outlook for the year, the meeting was opened for a discussion of problems left unsolved from the previous year. Continuation of the work on reading was suggested; one teacher expressed concern about the music reading program which she felt was inadequate; another hoped it would be possible to organize yard duty schedules more equitably; still another said she would like to know just how to deal with children and classroom situations in a democratic manner.

Considerable discussion indicated a recognition of the fact that many learning and control problems could be solved if teachers and administrators had more skills in democratic behavior. All other problems seemed to be subordinate to this and an agreement to study the "hows" of democratic behavior was reached. It was also decided to keep records of how the reading program, planned a year before, was working out and to consult the music supervisor regarding improvements in the music reading program.

Democratic Behavior in a Real Situation

At the next meeting of the group the question was raised, "All right, how *do* we behave more democratically?" Discussion followed regarding mutual respect, physical punishment that was "no good because it just didn't work," how hard it was to plan good experiences for children of widely varying abilities. Then a young woman in her second year of teaching spoke up, "I wish someone would tell me what to do with Abraham. I've tried everything I know and I've about given up." Other teachers contributed bits about Abraham—mostly bad. The suggestion was made that perhaps this might be a good spot to start studying democracy. "How will Miss L. deal with Abraham in a democratic manner?" The group had its problem.

This Is Abraham

The first step was to organize all the information obtainable about the boy. He was ten years old, in the fourth grade, and had entered this school for the first time in the fall. He had first gone into the third grade, as his report from a southern school had indicated this placement, but was sent within a few days to the fourth. He had been absent when the mental maturity and achievement tests had been given so the group had no objective data. He was living with his father and stepmother in "an awful place." The lad had had contacts, mostly unpleasant, with many of the teachers, so when it was decided to draw up a list of his assets and liabilities there was full participation.

Abraham's Assets	Abraham's Liabilities
Looks healthy (no one knew for sure)	Very low academic rating (can't do anything)
Is clean (someone must care about him)	Doesn't bring a lunch, but has money for candy
Is curious (an asset?)	Very poor in sports
Prints beautifully	Aggressive; other children don't like him

Then a list of reasons why Abraham behaves as he does was compiled.

Gets bored because he cannot do the school work
May be hungry in the afternoon
Cannot play games
Lives with his stepmother and his father. He may be emotionally insecure due to the home situation.

The next step was to plan for some positive action on what could be done about Abraham.

Get his I. Q. and his achievement rating on standardized tests
Have the nurse examine him for physical defects
Assign an older boy to help him develop some skills in games
Recheck his reading and arithmetic program to see if he is getting some opportunity for success
Give him some opportunities to use his skill in printing
Visit the home.

The teacher readily accepted the suggestions and contributed some herself. She expressed some insecurity about visiting the home. Abraham is a colored boy and she had never been in a Negro home. There were some suggestions and reassurances by the principal and the supervisor, both of whom had visited in homes in the Negro district. Thus the group moved to a related problem, "How to help Miss L. plan her interview with the parent."

It was suggested that a note asking if a certain time would be convenient should be sent in advance of the visit, and also that the visit should be made during school hours when children would not be present.

At this point it was decided to do some role-playing in this situation. How would the stepmother feel? How would Miss L. feel? The supervisor played the role of the mother, and another teacher played Miss L.'s part.

These Are Ways to Act

This led to a discussion of how little real acquaintance the group had with the realities of life in the Negro section of town. The feelings of the people, their housing and employment problems, and their church life were all practically unknown quantities to the teaching group. So it was decided to invite the Negro principal of a four-teacher school in a neighboring county to attend the next group meeting. Two of the four teachers in this school are white and two are colored. The school population is almost all colored. It was thought that the principal might have some insight on teaching problems which would be very valuable.

The invitation was accepted. The visiting principal knew the local situation well through friends who lived there. She had taught in the South and so was able to suggest adjustments Abraham would have to make. She had understanding of both the school and the family problems. Her presentation was well received and the discussion was lively. At this meeting refreshments were served and the situation was a very pleasant one.

At the following meeting Miss L. reported on her visit to Abraham's home. It had been very different than she had expected. Although the house was poor and most inadequate for the people living there, it was clean and some efforts had been made to make it attractive. Abraham's stepmother was also a surprise. She was a nice appearing, fairly well-educated woman. Miss L. said she gathered that the stepmother resented somewhat having to care for Abraham and his two brothers and one sister. Her own children were grown up, and this second family of "steps" was a burden. On the whole, however, she was cooperative, promised to send lunches with the children, and to help in other ways.

Consultation Leads To Action on Community Concerns

Discussion of Abraham's house led to general talk concerning the housing situation of the town. A survey taken a few years before had stated that sixty-eight percent of the houses were substandard. Since the teachers knew little about the housing situation, it was decided to invite the attendance supervisor from the county office to meet with the group and report on a state meeting which she had recently attended on the effect of poor housing on juvenile delinquency. Following the discussion of her report it was decided to write a letter to the state representative, asking that he support legislation to improve housing for low-income groups. A member of the group who belongs to the county division of the Republican Women's Organization agreed to bring the housing problems before that group.

The teachers discovered that many of the factors responsible for Abraham's difficulties were present in the problems of other children and that "it makes no difference if the children are black or white." Home and community problems were also school problems. Following up the proposals for solving Abraham's problems would help them solve the problems of other children. Through identifying Abraham's problems, the teachers found two new problems which they needed to start work on immediately? How could they work with the community on the housing problem? How could they develop a more democratic atmosphere in the classroom so that those children who felt no security at home might develop a feeling of "we-ness" at school?

Learning to Use Community Resources in City Schools

When the school system of Pasadena, California embarked upon a program of utilizing community resources, it soon became obvious that such a program was dependent upon fine public relations. As the program developed it became clear that the use of community resources in turn can become a significant contributor to the furthering of understanding and good will.

In developing the program for using community resources, group processes played an important part. First, many group meetings were held for the purpose of clarifying goals. In these meetings ideas were freely shared by teachers and supervisors and, in turn, screened against the general philosophy of the Pasadena City Schools. From these meetings there emerged a felt need for enrichment of the units of work. A desire to make the school experience more real and vital was evident, and as time went on the school itself was looked upon as an integral part of a larger process known as community living.

Children and Teachers Do Planning

Group process also involves pupils and teachers working together. It is a learning situation for both the teacher and child. In order to prepare the class and help it to make the best use of any particular community resource, the teacher must learn as much as possible about the situation. To do this a pre-excursion visit is very desirable. She must be able to establish an atmosphere of anticipation for the pupils so that they will be prepared for maximum participation. This point can be illustrated by presenting a typical chart developed by a teacher and a class previous to visiting the harbor.

What We Want to See at the Harbor

The work boats such as freighters, tankers, and tugs
The pilot boat
The fire boat
The warehouses where cargo is stored
The ships
The docks
The people who work at the harbor

Participation on the part of pupils is defined in very broad terms. The pupil is not only taught what to look for, but is also encouraged to use all of his five senses. If children are to develop an awareness to complete life situations they must be sensitive to smells, sounds, tastes, and textural sensations as well as visual experiences. All this requires that the teacher know ahead of time what things may be observed by all the senses.

After a visit to a harbor the teacher and pupils talk about what they saw. They also recall what they heard, such as the fog horn, the whistle of the tug, boxes and cargo as they are loaded, the rushing back and forth on the deck, signals, and people talking. The class reviews the smells experienced, such as the salty air, the smell of oil, the fish odors, rubber, hemp, bananas, and pineapples. All of these vital experiences become motivating forces for all the classroom activities. The pupils compose songs, they build harbors and boats for dramatic play, they paint posters, and they write and tell stories. The result is that learning is lifted out of a drab, uninteresting environment and established in a dynamic, creative one.

If the use of a particular community resource is to be achieved by an excursion, the teacher gives the class some guidance in knowing what to look for and to observe. Each pupil is prepared to look for all those things which are minimum basic elements related to the unit of work. In addition, each pupil is encouraged to select those elements which appeal to him especially in terms of his own interests and abilities. This promotes or provides common learnings plus individual uniqueness which can be shared with others.

Layman Share in the Process

To make a community resource readily available to schools for the purpose of enriching the school program requires still another aspect of group process involving numerous individuals. After the curriculum committees have decided upon the types of resources best suited to the instructional needs, someone must contact those in charge and make the necessary arrangements. The Pasadena experience indicates that this can best be done by one central agency, and a member of the Board of Education has assumed these activities as part of his public relations responsibilities.

Those in charge of a resource must first be contacted. The important objective here is to educate the owners or managers of these enterprises as to their responsibilities toward furthering the goals of the school program. Value is placed upon the importance of the contribution they can make.

A second problem is to develop together some sound procedures which will insure maximum educational values and at the same time prevent the dislocation of the regular routine of the shop, farm, or plant that may be involved in any particular excursion. These plans include considerations for transportation, guidance and supervision of pupils, rest room facilities, and provisions for food and water. Experience in Pasadena indicates that with this kind of cooperative planning the community at large is willing and anxious to help the schools.

After the details are worked out with those participating in the program, the teachers and pupils discuss together problems of behavior and conduct. Attitudes of interest, cooperation, and appreciation are stressed. The transportation problem can best be solved by use of public carriers. However, there are times when private cars are used. At these times careful planning is required with parents. Special techniques are developed to protect the children, and simple rules are agreed upon. These, in turn, must be adequately explained to the pupils in order to avoid liability in case of accident.

Community resources consist not only of factories, shops, farms, and public places, but also of mature adults who, from their rich experiences, have much to share with pupils. The so-called resource visitor can provide a valuable liaison between the real world and the theoretical world of the textbook. This type of activity needs to be carefully supervised.

Not all persons are adequate, and the schools must at all times be on guard against undesirable propaganda.

The use of resource visitors as well as the use of excursions is accompanied by a carefully developed evaluation program. The evaluation includes a study of the resource in terms of the goals and objectives of the class as well as a study of procedures used to make the resources a valuable, enriching experience for children.

Committees Operate at the Secondary Level

The above discussion has described briefly the procedures and methods of utilizing community resources in Pasadena City Schools on the elementary level. While many teachers on the secondary level have made a wide use of community resources, there has never been a systematic approach in terms of a total program. Supervisors and teachers alike have felt a need for more adequate use of resources, and to meet this desire a new Community Survey Committee has been appointed. The appointment of the Community Survey Committee represents a unique development of a group process which Pasadena has encouraged. The curriculum development on the secondary level is organized in terms of four major divisions: Applied Arts, Fine Arts, Natural Sciences, and Humanities. Each division has a Curriculum Coordinating Committee.

The Curriculum Coordinating Committees include parent representation. From time to time, as the need develops, production committees are appointed. These usually are within a given Division. The Community Survey Committee is an exception. The problem or need for a survey was first expressed in the Fine Arts Curriculum Coordinating Committee. It was not long, however, before several of the other Coordinating Committees expressed a desire to join in the study with the result that the final production committee includes members from two other Divisions. This way of working is a good demonstration of a group process which makes it possible for those with similar needs to get together and, by cooperative means, to do a much more effective piece of work.

This committee has three objectives: (a) to inventory the desires of teachers and students regarding the types of resources considered most desirable in terms of classroom units of work; (b) to find the resources desired and to enlist the cooperation of those controlling the resources; and (c) to prepare a teachers' handbook or file which will set forth the necessary information about the various resources and will give definite procedures to follow in order to make the resources readily available for classroom use. This project represents a next step in an on-going program which has, for many years, placed value upon the enrichment of learning experiences.

Planning and Decision Involve Many Individuals

In summary, attention should be called to the various group processes involved in utilizing community resources. First, there was the process of involving teachers and supervisors in the problem of thinking through educational goals and discussing ways to attain them. This was then followed by group effort involving both school and lay persons in developing plans and working relationships, which would make possible the wide participation of many people and agencies in enriching the school program. Finally, there was the process of reaching decisions on how to proceed in order to develop good classroom procedures, which would insure maximum learning on the part of the pupils.

Learning To Use Community Resources in Rural Schools

The teachers of Lassen County, California worked together for a year in making a survey of community resources. A number of supervisory problems had led to the initiation of this project by the county staff. A new framework for the social studies adopted by the state called for the development of a great deal of new resource material for teachers. It was hoped that this new material would make use of community resources to a far greater extent than before, vitalizing both curriculum content and teaching procedures.

A need was also felt to draw the teachers of the county more closely together for mutual inspiration and assistance. Schools in each of the principal communities had been operating with very little interchange of ideas, partly because of distance in this mountain area and the long snow season, and partly because there had been no county supervision in these centers to facilitate interaction. There was no county course of study, and the staff was looking for an opportunity to start building one which would be based soundly on the thinking of the teachers.

After considerable discussion among themselves and with teacher groups, the supervisory staff came to these conclusions. It seemed obvious that a large group undertaking was indicated. It would have to be a project which teachers would consider valuable, because of an evident need or because of its contribution to their own work. It should be based on a problem which could be attacked better by the joint efforts of the whole group than by any individual; it should not be a job for experts. It should be broad enough to utilize the peculiar talents and abilities of many people.

A Community Handbook Becomes the Point of Approach

Compiling material for a handbook of community resources was selected as a promising enterprise. The first steps were tentative, all designed to find out whether the project interested teachers. A number of teachers in the county had been using community resources extensively for several years. Others had made some initial uses of excursions and speakers early in the year, following individual conferences with supervisors in planning their units. At faculty meetings in the separate communities during October, forms were given to all teachers with the request that they report the resources they had used or knew would be available to the schools. It was explained that this material was to be gathered together and organized into a reference handbook so that all teachers might share the information, eliminating the necessity for each teacher to spend valuable time in working alone to find such resources for her own use.

The teachers who had used community resources recognized the value of having this information readily available to them and were ready to cooperate in pooling the information they had already obtained. Some of the others seemed interested, also, and made contributions. Distribution of this questionnaire served to focus the attention of all teachers on the fact that there were community resources available to them which could be of real value in their work. It was felt, also, that a beginning was made in group feeling with the recognition that the teachers of the entire area shared common problems and might cooperate for mutual benefit.

Organizing Material Is the First Group Task

Approximately one hundred reports were returned. The first group work was the organization of this material. A committee of teachers representing the various sections of the county was appointed. This committee, organizing the reports according to the general area of community life to which each applied, found that many worth-while and easily accessible resources had not been included in this random gathering of material. The group decided that, though the handbook should be loose-leaf and subject to easy revision and addition, it should be as complete as possible in its first publication. To fill in the gaps, the general committee planned an organized survey, appointing subcommittees for each important aspect of community life which needed to be covered: transportation, communication, history, government, public utilities, protective services, agriculture, lumbering, forestry, recreation, business and industry, community organizations, and local science materials. Each of these subcommittees included members from the various areas of the county so that the material could be collected in each locality by persons in the best position to know and reach sources.

Committees Carry Through

To each subcommittee was sent a letter explaining the survey project and asking for cooperation, a list of the committee appointments, and a specific description of the work being requested from that committee. As an example of the specific instructions outlined, the letter to the committee on lumbering asked that individual forms be filled out for each of the principal mills in the county; for persons who would be willing to speak to the children about lumbering operations; for persons whom the children might interview; and for moving pictures, still picture collections, exhibits, and other visual materials available in the county. The committee was asked to check each resource so reported to be sure that the persons concerned were willing to cooperate with the schools, and to find out about any limitations or requirements as to time, size of group, or other factors. In addition to these reports on individual resources, the committee was asked for a descriptive summary of lumbering in the county, showing the extent and character of operations and containing such other information as would be valuable to a new teacher coming into the county.

The fact that committee members were scattered over the county at some distance from one another, though advantageous from the standpoint of gathering material and providing wide representation, had the disadvantage of making group meetings difficult. To get the work started well, the general committee then planned a county-wide professional meeting in February, a few days after the above material was sent out.

A General Meeting Is Necessary

This meeting included a general session on community resources, followed by meetings of each of the survey committees. The general session presentation was made by a panel of three teachers, a principal, and the supervisors. The program included a report by the handbook committee on the survey which had just been started; a discussion of the techniques involved in the field trip by one of the teachers who was widely experienced and successful in using excursions; a discussion of the best methods for using resource persons by another teacher; a talk by a principal on opportunities for children to participate in community activities; and a supervisor's discussion of planning classroom experiences to precede and follow the use of community resources, with an exhibit of materials developed by teachers with their classes. Mimeographed suggestions for use of the field trip, resource persons, and service projects were distributed at this meeting. Following the meeting, the handbook committee decided that outlines of these techniques should be incorporated in the handbook for ready reference.

The survey committees then met to outline and organize their tasks and to distribute responsibilities. Some committees had follow-up meetings, but much of the cooperative work had to be carried on by mail.

The final work of collecting the material, organizing and unifying it, and filling in missing data was done by the general committee late in the school year. The manuscript was printed during the summer and distributed to teachers during the fall conference preceding the opening of school. In its final form it included five sections: (a) a general overview of community life in Lassen County, (b) a survey of the features of natural environment, (c) an alphabetical listing of the resources available for use in the school program, (d) an index to resources for each unit of study, and (e) a section suggesting techniques for using community resources.

Strengths Outweigh Weaknesses

Obviously the chief weakness of this project was in the limited amount of face-to-face group planning and action. The most effective work was done during such meetings, and it would have been extremely desirable to increase these opportunities if that had been possible. By far the best group thinking was done by the general committee, which continued its work through a number of meetings over a period of an entire year.

However, the project was certainly successful for the entire teacher group. As a group, these teachers experienced the satisfaction of carrying through a valuable piece of work which could not have been produced without this joint action. Practically every teacher in the county can point to some part of the handbook as her own contribution. As a result, here is definitely increased awareness of group membership, as well as greater acceptance of the value of group processes and a favorable tendency toward their use.

Leadership Eases the Process

The role of leadership in this enterprise was simply that of facilitating the work of groups. Some member of the supervisory staff met with the general committee for each of its meetings and participated in the planning. This leadership provided follow-up at each step to see that work was proceeding in each committee, to clear obstacles, to help organize and define the tasks, to revive flagging enthusiasm. As many persons as possible were drawn into the work and the supervisors made it their business to see that all contributions were used. It was felt that the success of the project depended on the amount of satisfaction which resulted for each participant, and, as leaders, the supervisors attempted to make participation as wide and as successful as possible.

Studying Children and the Social Structure of Classrooms

A group of about fifty teachers interested in the work of the fourth, fifth, and sixth grades worked together on source units as part of an in-service program. The work was done in small committees, with the groups pooling their ideas for art, music, science, and other experiences that might contribute to the general social studies unit. As activities were suggested the group became increasingly aware of the need to develop criteria for evaluating them. The major bases for the selection of experiences follow: Do they fit what we know about the physical, mental, social, and emotional growth characteristics of children of this age group? Have we provided activities for children of widely differing maturity and talents? Are the learning situations effective in the light of what we know about how children learn? Are basic human needs adequately met?

Knowledge of the social structure of a class group was considered important in relation to each of these criteria. Studies in child growth indicate that certain intergroup patterns are typical in the intermediate grades, but that these will vary with the particular group and can be modified. There are great individual differences in the degree to which children are accepted by the others in a class. To the degree that learning involves the whole child in the total situation, the social structure is an important ingredient in each experience.

Sociograms Provide a Means of Approach

Seven teachers took on the task of constructing sociograms of their classes. After reading articles on the use of sociograms they planned the particular method to be used. They decided to ask each child to write the name of his best friend and then the names of two other very good friends in the class. Each child was also asked to name the class member he did not wish to sit near. The teachers were concerned that the problem be presented in such a way that it would not make for ill-feeling in the class. The confidential nature of the information was stressed, but it was decided that each teacher, taking into account her own personality and the general group tone of her class, would devise her own method for getting the information.

A case was selected for special analysis from each of the seven sociograms. Those chosen included a girl and a boy who were leaders or stars in their groups; two rejected girls, one of high intelligence and pleasing appearance, the other unattractive and of low intelligence; a boy and a girl who were neither chosen as friends nor actively rejected; and a clique of three girls. Over a period of several weeks the teachers watched these children and wrote anecdotes of those situations that might throw light on the position of each child in his group. These were collected and mimeographed so that everyone could have them to refer to when the sociograms were presented.

Means of Sharing Information Are Devised

A problem existed in getting the sociograms clearly before such a large group. To solve this difficulty they were prepared in the form of large wall charts. The cases to be given particular attention were marked in color. Each teacher gave a thumbnail sketch of the child from her class with emphasis on making the child "come alive" for the others in the group. These sketches were highly successful. There were many chuckles as the teachers recognized counterparts of children they had in their own classes.

A surprisingly free discussion followed each presentation in spite of the fact that the group had grown to include about seventy persons. Suggestions were made concerning possible causes of the child's social adjustment and of other kinds of information that the teacher ought to have. Steps which the teacher might take to improve adjustment were considered, and the total structures were discussed in terms of how a group might be helped toward better adjustment. Almost every teacher went away from the meetings realizing the importance of knowing the social structure of her classroom and with a knowledge of how to improve social relations. Sociograms were one of the tools which the teachers in attendance now knew how to use advantageously.

Evaluating Changes in Pupil Behavior

Gerald was in trouble. He had been found prowling the streets late at night in the company of high school boys. He had broken into a store, taken cigarettes and several lighters, and the next day had sold them to his friends. The sheriff had come for Gerald at school. Gerald was seated sullenly in the principal's office. He was a big boy for twelve, muscular shoulders and large hands hanging from his coat sleeves. "He's like all the rest," said the sheriff. "There's a bunch of them that just roam the streets looking for trouble. If their parents can't control them, I don't know what we can do."

For this principal it was time for action, not for complaint about modern youth nor for punishment of the culprit. He persuaded the officer to hold off for a few days while the school got into action. He needed information. Gerald was not in the mood to give much, and the school records were full of cold figures that did not answer his questions. So Mr. Newhoff called the school nurse, Gerald's teacher, and his teacher of the year before and told them the story. They agreed to do some investigating, to think about his interests, to observe him on the playground and in the classroom, and to give him some tests that might be revealing. He then made an appointment with the school psychologist to see Gerald, and he himself started for Gerald's home.

The Problem Goes to the Group

A week later a meeting was called for all teachers who were interested in the problem. Every teacher came because they all knew Gerald or had heard about his difficulty. Some were curious, but most of them wanted to help. The purpose of the meeting was clear—to discover the cause of Gerald's behavior and to plan a course of action to help him.

The psychologist was chosen as leader of the group because she was able to interpret the information and to give insight into the dynamics of behavior. The nurse presented the medical report. Gerald was advanced in his development, mature and large for his age, well coordinated and strong. He had wet his bed since he had been five years old. To the teachers this meant poor training. The psychologist reported on research which showed that bed wetting usually stemmed from an emotional disturbance often rooted in the relationship between mother and child.

His teacher said that he was a good student but had no zest for his work. He did what he was told and that was all. He read books in his free time—comic books and the western cowboy variety. He was good in sports; played basketball particularly well, but was so cocky and overbearing on the playground that the other boys resented him. She had made a sociogram to discover more about his relationships to the others in the group. Out of a possible 105 friendship choices, only one boy had chosen Gerald as his third choice. No girl in this sixth grade had shown interest in him. He was quiet in the classroom, having difficulty only on the playground with the other boys. He had occasionally been impudent to the teacher on the yard when he had been corrected or disciplined.

Gerald's teacher of last year reported that he had had many more conflicts with the children in her class, but that he had made more of an effort to be a part of the group. He wanted to be noticed—and even to lead. It was noticeable this year, she said, that he seemed preoccupied and withdrawn from his classmates.

Information Is Gathered First Hand

Mr. Newhoff, the principal, had visited the home. Gerald lived with his mother, stepfather, and two stepsisters in a trailer on a used car lot. The father bought used cars and reconditioned them for sale. There was no room for Gerald to sleep in the trailer, so he had his bed in a little office at the rear of the lot, an easy place to slip out of without being noticed. A used car lot, a trailer, and a little office were not very adequate for a husky twelve-year-old, nor was there any place to play or entertain one's friends.

The mother had told Mr. Newhoff this story: Gerald's father had died when he was a year old. The mother and son were inseparable until he was five, when she married again. They soon had two little girls with whom Gerald quarreled interminably. The stepfather was fond of Gerald but exasperated by his unwillingness to sand paint from the old cars and help around the lot. "He always wants to be on the move," said his stepfather, "but for no good reason. He talks about wanting to be a pilot or a cowboy or an engineer, but I tell him he'll never amount to anything unless he learns how to work now." The mother and stepfather had tried all sorts of punishments and rewards to keep him home and make him pay attention to his work. Mr. Newhoff had known Gerald for only a year and a half. He called his previous school and found that Gerald had been troublesome since kindergarten.

The psychologist reported her findings: intelligence, above average; response and cooperation, good; extreme jealousy of the younger sister and the father; devotion to, yet resentment of the mother. Gerald showed restlessness, energy which was undirected, and imagination. He felt unwanted by his family and by his classmates. His only close relationship was with the two high school boys who had been the inspiration of his unfortunate escapades.

The jigsaw puzzle was falling into place. The psychologist discussed the normal characteristics of twelve-year-olds—their need for independence and adventure, their strong desire to be part of the gang or group, their need for adult leadership and adult models as well as of family security. She discussed the effect of early emotional disturbances on later adjustment and how frustrations of normal drives lead to aggressive behavior. Teachers illustrated this theoretical material with examples from their own classrooms. One teacher said, "We might have been talking about my John instead of Gerald. The story is different but the facts are the same." Another commented, "I see now the importance of studying problems. It is only by studying mistakes that we can avoid them."

Analysis Leads to Action

The next step in the process was to identify all the causes of Gerald's behavior as clearly as possible and to outline a plan of action. All teachers contributed from their own experience. Elements in Gerald's problem were recognizable in many of their students, and they were eager to tell of their children's behavior and their methods of meeting the difficulties. The impossibility of reorganizing Gerald's whole life and creating a perfect environment for him was immediately apparent, yet they were eager to go to work and see what could be done.

The following analysis was made by the group: Gerald was extremely close to his mother for five years—then she married and had two babies, which made him feel left out. The father was a stern, hardworking man. Gerald interpreted this characteristic as rejection and dislike. Sleeping in the little office instead of the trailer was a further indication that he was not wanted, as was his mother's scolding when he quarreled with his sisters. Life was drab on the car lot; nothing but work and no opportunity to do the exciting things other boys did. His strong muscles, physical agility, and maturing body made him eager for interesting activity. Sleeping away from his family gave him the opportunity at night, that he lacked in the daytime, to experiment with adventure.

Some of the teachers blamed the parents for their ignorance and neglect. Others blamed the community for allowing trailer living and not supervising home conditions. Other teachers replied that, while there might be sociological or educational inadequacies in every community, placing blame was not profitable and did not relieve the school of responsibility as the only organized group capable of doing something to alleviate the problem. The suggestions for action and the delegation of responsibility were as follows:

> Mr. Newhoff agreed to talk to Gerald's father and to plan some better living arrangements. He would suggest a workshop, tools, and equipment for Gerald. He would talk to the minister to see if he might invite Gerald to the young peoples' group.
> The coach knew the Scout leader in the area. He would speak to him so that Gerald would be invited to join. The coach also agreed to organize an after-school basketball team. That might interest many of the boys.
> Gerald's teacher thought of many ways she might make the class-

room more interesting to him, and the other teachers poured out suggestions to her. A hobby club, science experiments, committee work were some of the ideas.

To build friendships for Gerald seemed to be a major issue. Many ideas were advanced: pair Gerald on a project with a boy of similar interests; seat him next to the boys in which he had shown the greatest friendliness; give him a job such as running the school projector, which would bring him prestige in the eyes of his group; allow him to referee games occasionally to increase his sportsmanship.

The psychologist agreed to talk with the parents to help them gain insight into the causes of Gerald's attitudes, and to plan some better ways of living at home.

All the teachers felt that their knowledge of Gerald would improve their incidental contacts with him at school and in the community. They felt, too, that their understanding of Gerald would help them in dealing with the children in their own classrooms. They left the meeting with many new ideas for improved teaching methods. They set a time the next month for an evaluation of progress, a revision of their suggestions.

Group Thinking Has Varied Results

The method described above appears to be an effective one for diagnosing and evaluating pupil behavior because of the following elements:

The goal was clear, and the means required to achieve the goal used the varied talents and knowledges of a number of individuals.

The heterogeneity of the group and the diversified opinions served to clarify the thinking of all. The teachers were willing to try out suggestions and arrive at tentative solutions for a difficult problem.

Because of the active interest of all teachers in this problem and their eagerness to do the right thing for a child in trouble, the method raised the level of thinking of all participants.

The leader was chosen by the group because of her special contribution in interpreting and coordinating the material. Leadership did not remain with the psychologist but was given from time to time to various group members whose knowledge and contribution placed them in a position of leadership and authority.

The results of the group thinking not only achieved the purpose of the group but permeated the thinking of all group members and affected the lives of many children through improved teaching techniques and greater understanding of child development.

Changing the Behavior of Teachers

Within Butte County there live some 3500 children, whose opportunities for educational instruction come under the leadership of the county superintendent of schools. To assist him in the execution of the educational program, there is a county staff of eight members and a county board of education. Under direct guidance of the county superintendent are forty-five elementary schools, over half of which are one-room country schools. There are 120 teachers, about one-third of whom are new each year. Aside from this group who need to be oriented there is a proportionate share who have not had the opportunity for recent training in a modern school program. The role of supervisor has thus become largely one of teacher education. Because of geographical distances, uniqueness of teaching situations, and differences in educational background, the problem of organizing teacher groups for study is most challenging.

During the school year 1946-47, it seemed that the need to raise the quality of teaching in the field of social studies was most urgent. The teachers, as a group, had had no opportunity to become familiar with the state department of education publication, *Implementation of the Framework of the Social Studies*.[3] This, it was felt, would serve as an excellent guide for a sound basis of procedure, although the needs of the county would require making many adaptations.

Like Problems Govern Formation of Subgroups

How to organize county teachers into working groups for the most effective participation then had to be considered. Since the teachers of multigraded schools have problems unlike other schools, it seemed logical that they might profit most by working together. Another group was formed representing teachers of two- and three-room schools. They, too, would have to make adaptations to the State Framework in terms of local needs. The third group was composed of teachers of the four-room schools or larger. They could adapt more readily to the recommended units from the Framework. Within each group, except for the teachers of multigraded schools, a further organization was made according to primary, intermediate, and upper-grade levels. Two meetings were held in the spring of 1947. One general supervisor served as leader for each subgroup. At the close of the school year every teacher had had the benefit of the group thinking so that she was able to bring to the County Office of Education a pre-plan which contained:

> The name of the unit to be taught for the coming year
>
> A suggestive list of questions under each area in the scope of the Framework that would be interesting to children at a given age level
>
> A list of related experiences children might engage in to satisfy the basic drives.
>
> A suggestive list of materials for a planned environment.

---

[3] Helen Heffernan, *Implementation of the Framework of the Social Studies in the Elementary Schools*. Sacramento: Division of Elementary Education, State Department of Education, June 1946.

Attention Is Given to Materials

Simultaneous to the development of the social studies program the general supervisor was given responsibility for the selection of new audio-visual materials, although plans were being made to add a director of audio-visual education to the staff. At that time it did not seem wise to ask the teachers to attend additional meetings to preview materials; however, upon a few occasions several teachers who lived within close distances volunteered to come to the office for that purpose.

During the summer, members of the supervisory staff took the initiative in organizing and compiling the pre-plans formerly submitted. One volunteer group meeting was called. At this time divisions in groups were made according to the units to be taught. The purpose of this meeting was two-fold: (a) to criticize and evaluate the pre-planning that had been compiled, and (b) to preview some related visual-aid materials and to see how and when they might be used most effectively.

Actually this was the first organized attempt to show the relationship between the social studies program and visual materials to be used. Despite the warm weather and the fact that many teachers were out of town, the meeting was well attended. Perhaps the greatest value gained from this meeting was that those present had become familiar with specific visual materials appropriate for a given unit of work.

The Program Continues

With the opening of school in the fall of 1947, the organization of the audio-visual department was well under way. A new director was in charge. All social studies materials purchased at that time were organized and catalogued, and the appropriate list was added to the pre-plans for each unit. In preparation for the opening of school three geographical area meetings were arranged. At each of these meetings the teachers were divided according to primary, intermediate, and upper-grade levels.

The same supervisors continued to work with the same group throughout the day. Meetings were held in schools where experienced teachers had set up planned environments. This afforded teachers the opportunity to see first hand what was meant by an arranged environment. Flat pictures, film strips, models, and other realia were a part of the physical surroundings. Within the county were over forty new teachers who had no identity with any of the work that had gone on before. Since this was the first time they had seen the pre-plan in its compiled form, it seemed worth-while to present the organization of it to the entire group again. The form, "Ways to Record the Progress of a Unit of Work," was introduced and its use discussed.

For a semester the teachers were concerned with the doing of the task. Help was given individually both by the general supervisor and the audio-visual director. New materials were being purchased, building coordinators were being selected, better darkening facilities were becoming more available, and teachers were visiting the department to have assistance in learning how to operate the equipment. These were contributing factors to the development and functional use of the program.

Evaluation Accompanies Progress

About the middle of the year, groups met again in order to make some evaluation of their progress. Those teaching the same unit formed the basis for the groups. The purpose of these meetings was three-fold:

—To encourage teachers to bring in all types of tangible evidences which indicated the variety of experiences children were having as a result of the work in social studies,
—To think through together the "Ways of Recording the Development of the Unit" for the benefit of those who needed help, and
—To show materials and discuss the classroom utilization of audio-visual materials.

Some of the teachers brought tangible evidences of friezes, cooperative stories, class booklets, and drawings which showed some of the ways materials were being used. This afforded an excellent opportunity to expand and project the idea of wider utilization of visual materials.

At the time this article was written there had been five group meetings. In view of emerging needs, they will continue. The content, taken from "Ways of Recording the Development of the Unit," will need to be screened and incorporated into the pre-plans for each unit of work. Again each teacher will wish to think through the needs of her children and plan next year's work accordingly.

New Considerations Emerge

Paralleling this need is the feeling that groups will be able to give serious consideration to discussing and demonstrating the kinds of experience children may engage in to satisfy their basic needs. The use of a variety of audio-visual materials serves as an excellent springboard for such experiences. *Materials, as such, are only worth-while as they relate and function in a total well-rounded program. They become the vehicles through which learning takes place. Other things being equal, better utilization means better learning.*

The following summarization, expressed by members within the group, indicate that teachers enjoy group meetings most when characterized by some of the following conditions and situations:

"It is easier to talk when the groups are kept small."
"I like to meet with teachers who are doing the same unit as I am doing. We have so much in common."
"It is interesting to see the charts, booklets, stories, paintings, and maps done by other children. It helps you check against your own teaching."
"I like to meet in different buildings; to see the actual room environment. You get good ideas."
"Saturday morning meetings, if not held too often, are fun. At least, you are not so tired as you are after school."
"Yes, the serving of light refreshments helps to make an informal atmosphere."
"These last meetings have been more help to me than any I have attended for a long time. I am going to spend my entire summer next year getting ready."
"I wouldn't be happy going back to the old way of teaching, but I never could have changed over by myself."
"Slowly but surely I am beginning to understand. It has been a slow process but these meetings have certainly helped me. This last one has been the best of all."

The Supervisor Has a Three-Fold Task

Since the group process can only be achieved in a healthy emotional climate, the supervisor *tried to be extremely sensitive to all forces which influenced the feeling tones of the group.* This implied:

> Having a genuine regard and appreciation for the worth of each individual and a willingness to understand and accept each one at his own level of growth.
> Making a plan of organization but at no time adhering to it so rigidly that the wishes, expression, and attitudes of the group were not considered.
> A willingness and open-mindedness on the part of the group leader so that differences of opinion could be expressed without an emotional display.

Because the supervisor was also concerned with better materials and better instructional practices she felt *the challenge to be informed.*

This required: screening and selecting materials in terms of needs, relatedness, and quality; a willingness to learn how to use all equipment sufficiently well to serve her use or purpose; and a willingness to demonstrate techniques and methods in the use of such materials in classrooms.

At all times there was the felt need on the part of the supervisor for *self-evaluation.*

This called forth the desire: (a) to re-think and re-state her own set of values in order that she herself would recognize worth-while purposes to be achieved; (b) to review the psychology of learning and to apply it in terms of the growth levels of the group; (c) to consult with other staff members, both before and after the meetings, to clarify basic thinking; and (d) to try at all times to visualize the total program through the eyes of the classroom teacher.

Learning To Use the Problem-Solving Method

Each spring, as the school year draws to a close, teachers, principals, supervisors, and educational psychologists sit together to appraise achievements of the year, to plan for professional summer activities, and to consider ways of improving the instructional program for the year ahead.

Last spring there were informal conferences in fourteen neighborhood schools of a rural section of Los Angeles County. Some of the conferences involved two or three teachers, while others involved a staff of from six to fourteen teachers. In each conference teachers noted areas of progress during the current year; they talked about their own teaching experiences and ways in which they felt such experiences could have been more beneficial to children and more satisfying to themselves. They talked about teacher education opportunities available to them through their local districts, through county supervisory services, and through university extension classes. They expressed their hopes and ambitions with regard to the improvement of education in the schools in which they were teaching.

Means of Growth Are Suggested and Organized

These teachers identified topics and problems which they felt should be given further study. They suggested ways in which they and the many new teachers who would join them the following fall could continue to study together. They asked their principals and supervisors to set up institutes, workshops, and area meetings to consider a large number of specific topics. They asked specifically that an extension class be organized to consider rural school curriculum adaptations.

The supervisor and the psychologist who serve these rural schools were present at all of the conferences. Following meetings in the fourteen individual schools, a representative committee met with the supervisor and psychologist to plan a specific in-service education program. Institute sessions were scheduled; field services were planned; the extension course was organized by the state university.

Experience Is Based on Group Needs

September came. Forty teachers registered for the extension class to study problems in curriculum and instruction under the leadership of a county supervisor. At the first meeting the leader invited the teachers to help plan the content and procedures to be followed during the eighteen ensuing meetings. Specific problems or questions listed for consideration in the spring conferences were reviewed. Some of the teachers most concerned in April and May had moved cityward. Several teachers in the September group were new to the profession or to their situation. A few of the original questions were eliminated. New or additional topics were listed on the blackboard; they were discussed and classified. Some of the questions were of a routine or informational nature and could be answered immediately by referring the inquirer to printed sources. Others were of such significance as to be of concern throughout the entire year.

At the close of the initial discussion period, the following significant problems and questions had been redefined for study:

> How can teachers new to their situations become acquainted with the children in rural communities in which they are teaching?
> How can teachers come to know their communities well enough to make appropriate curriculum adaptation?
> Should teachers teach what they believe to be important and right or what the school board and parents tell them to teach?
> Should teachers use the methods they know best or teach the way the supervisor wants them to teach?
> Which is the more important: social studies or the skills?
> What are considered to be good methods in teaching the social studies?
> How can we learn to use problem-solving methods in teaching the social studies without neglecting reading, writing, spelling, and arithmetic?
> Why are there so many ideas of what ought to be taught and how to teach? Why can't teachers get together? Wouldn't it be a good thing to have state laws to make all schools teach the same thing in the same grades?
> What can a teacher do when over half the class isn't up to grade standards?
> Why do children misbehave? Isn't there too much freedom in school nowadays?
> Why is it that children who come from other states seem to excel our children in the skills?
> How can we evaluate pupil growth?

The reader will readily recognize a logical pattern for the organization of a regular extension course. But this was not to be a regular course—it was to be a course built around problems agreed upon by the group, and so the group made a tentative schedule. They modified the schedule a number of times as discussions began to show interrelationships. Some members of the group were reluctant to change the original schedule because it permitted them to see where they were going. Others said they felt the instructor should have made the outline in the first place and "kept us at it so we would finish all that we are supposed to finish in this course." Other members of the group expressed surprise to find that a course could be made to "hang together without just one textbook from which to take our assignments." And some said, "This helps us to see some sense in a unit. Funny, isn't it, how everything relates to everything else?"

The Group Is the Laboratory

The remainder of this description will be confined to a specific example of what was done to help answer questions related to teaching the social studies.

> How can we as teachers learn to use more effective methods in teaching the social studies?
> What is a unit of work?
> To what extent can a teacher trained in formal methods be expected to use the problem-solving method?
> How can one learn to use this approach?

Such were the questions posed. Several selected references were discussed. A professional bookshelf was made available. A volunteer librarian issued books. Plans for the next session were to include a presentation of points of view and trends, followed by group discussion.

The class of forty adults met in an eighth-grade classroom. Movable desks arranged in rows faced the front of the room, where the teacher's desk occupied a central spot. A presentation on the content and organization of the social studies was given, after which there was a discussion period.

Near the close of the session the leader asked, "If this were your classroom and you had just completed a discussion period such as the one we have experienced tonight, how would you evaluate the day's work?"

There was a pause, then laughter.

"Do you mean it?" asked one member of the group.

"When should one evaluate progress?" countered the instructor.

The group made the following observations:

"We couldn't always hear what other members of the class were saying."

"Some members of the class didn't participate at all."

"Some said too much without saying anything of importance."

"Some of us didn't know enough about what we were supposed to be discussing."

"There wasn't a definite assignment."

"The instructor let us express too many ideas without telling us whether we were right or wrong."

Not all members of the group agreed with all of the points raised in discussion; however, it was decided that there should be changes in discussion techniques and room arrangement.

When the class met a week later, questions relative to using the scientific method in teaching the social studies were recorded on the blackboard, with subpoints which the group had listed the previous week. There was a brief review of the suggestions resulting from class evaluation of the previous discussion period. Seating was rearranged in the form of an open square. The function and characteristics of a discussion period and the respective roles of leader and participants were discussed.

After preliminary planning the group continued its deliberation of significant questions about the social studies. It became apparent that objectives, content, and organization of social studies were of vital concern to all members of the group. They still wanted to learn about method, but they found that the interrelationship between content and method made it imperative that the process not be rushed.

To present an overview of the several steps in problem-solving and to illustrate the interrelationship, the group chose the subquestion, "How can teachers new to Antelope Valley become acquainted with and make use of community resources?" On the blackboard they recorded:

> Who is involved in acquainting teachers with the resources of the valley?
> What information is already available?
> What do we need to know and what are the sources of information?
> What are the ways of acquainting teachers with resources of the valley?
> What are the ways of organizing information for use of new teachers?
> How can we use resources to enrich the curriculum?
> How can we evaluate what we decide to do?

As a direct outgrowth of the discussion of the use of community resources it was decided that committees would (a) investigate resources of the valley, (b) compile a community-resource record form, (c) record data about each resource on the card form, (d) set up a resource file in each school of the valley, (e) compile a handbook for teachers and parents new to the valley. Thus, through an experience used to illustrate a procedure, the group developed enthusiasm for a project which would help them directly in their classroom work, and which would result in a cumulative resource file to be kept up to date and used by fellow teachers over a period of years. As the discussion proceeded, main points were outlined; the leader summarized from time to time and injected questions to stimulate further reaction.

Near the close of the session the group again evaluated its experience. Some members frankly stated that they felt confused and would like to have a book assignment. Several seventh- and eighth-grade teachers in the group decided to try similar procedures with children in their own classrooms on topics and questions of particular interest to children.

Discussion Techniques Are Identified

At the end of the session the group was helped to summarize pertinent comments and observations relative to the use of the discussion technique. These were recorded for further reference and use as the class progressed during the term.

- In answering any question or solving any problem it is essential that the meaning of the question be clearly understood.
- Questions are not necessarily problems.
- A big over-all problem may include many smaller or more immediate aspects of the problem.
- In solving any problem it is essential to have accurate information about the present status of the situation and why it is as it is, what other teachers have found to be true about the same problem, what the experts say, what the research has proven, why the problem is a problem.
- Information may come from a wide variety of sources: from experience, from observation, from talking with others, from listening, from reading, from experimentation, from films.
- The best way to clarify questions, to share information, and to plan next steps is through the use of group discussion. Discussion should lead to action. Some questions or problems require long periods of study, whereas others may be solved in a short amount of time. Sometimes there is a tendency to spend so much time getting information that individuals or groups fail to evaluate its use or to apply it in meaningful situations.
- Tentative decisions or conclusions should be tried out before they become final. In many situations there may be more than one solution.
- Individuals can learn to be proficient in discussion only through opportunity to discuss and through the evaluation of group techniques in relation to their own activities.

During the several sessions which followed, demonstrations of the use of a variety of sources of information were arranged such as: experimentation, films, observation of children at work, reading, reporting, listening, interviewing, reading charts, graphs, and maps.

Each class session was conducted in a manner similar to that appropriate in the elementary school. Members of the group were learning group processes and how to use the many enrichment materials and techniques by actually using them in their own class work.

When it came time to organize data, the committee on community resources outlined on charts their findings from interviews, observations, and reading. They prepared a report on the history, industries, and activities of the people of various parts of the valley; made maps and compiled a handbook for teachers and parents. Thus they have experienced another important step in the scientific method.

The Group Identifies Aspects of Growth

Throughout the course there were opportunities to evaluate techniques in terms of individual and group purposes. Some of the most significant evidences of growth were:

- In beginning sessions each participant spoke in turn with little or no interaction among members of the group. After four or five experiences (two and a half hours at a time), there was a shift to a quick exchange of ideas, interjection of questions, some refutation, requests for documentation, and rebuttal. In the beginning about one-fifth of the group were active participants. At the close of the course less than a fifth of the class were vocally inactive.
- Individuals became less conscious of who said what, and showed more concern over questions and issues.
- Points on which there were differences of opinion were seldom challenged in the beginning sessions, except by the leader. In later sessions an unsubstantiated generalization was pounced upon with enthusiasm.
- Participants reported that they had read more professional literature under this plan than where textbooks and reading are assigned.
- A number of teachers reported successful attempts to use problem-solving techniques in their own classrooms. A few teachers reported upon attempts which were not satisfying and successful. Analyses were made and suggestions for improvement listed.
- There was an increasing tendency on the part of the members of the group to request clarification or explanation of points leading toward generalization. They became more discriminating in their use of generalizations.
- In early sessions members of the group tended to hold a defensive or protective attitude toward the techniques employed in problem situations. As the group worked together over a period of time there was a shift to analysis of those situations which, despite best effort, were not satisfactorily solved.
- In an analysis of the classroom activities provided children in their own classrooms, teachers were frank to admit that they had made no provision for many of the significant learning and enrichment experiences.

- There was evidence of greater progress in the ability to discuss and to use the variety of procedures on an adult level than in carrying the same procedures into their own classrooms.

Several leadership roles emerged, beginning with the initial conferences at which teachers had opportunity to identify their own problems and plan procedures for receiving help in the solution of their problems. The supervisor, psychologist, and administrators who provided opportunity for teachers to explore their needs freed them to contribute their best thinking toward the solution of their common problems. These status leaders did not hesitate to enlist the help of outside resources; they did not give answers to the many questions teachers asked—rather they helped to provide experiences through which teachers found their own answers. They retained membership in the group.

During the course the instructor as status leader shared a major responsibility for maintaining a climate of free communication, summarizing, pointing up issues needing further consideration, drawing implications, and furnishing documentary data. However, during discussion periods teachers within the group emerged in leadership roles with increasing frequency. They pointed up issues needing further consideration; they helped to determine the direction of activity; they were quick to appraise progress; and they evaluated the soundness of the philosophy and practice developed in the education course in terms of experiences in their own classrooms.

Releasing the Unique Talents and Abilities of Individual Teachers

A large school system had become somewhat ingrown as a result of comparatively little turn-over in personnel. For a number of years the administrative and supervisory staffs had been set apart from the teaching staff and deep feelings of "they" against "us" had grown up. Only those in the higher salary brackets were recognized as able to carry forward the tasks, make the decisions, and demonstrate the varied techniques of guiding children to better ways of learning and doing. Only certain and particular ways of doing things were thought to be acceptable. In the years that had passed some of the supervisory service had been authoritarian, exact, dreaded, and cold. The experiences with this type of supervision had colored all the actions and attitudes toward supervision. As a result of this relationship teachers had become timid, fearful, and distrustful of their own abilities. It was a "tell me what you want me to do" sort of attitude if teachers did agree to any request that involved teaching when other adults were present. It was safer to refuse to assume a responsibiltiy which might bring growth and increased prestige . . . and so satisfactions . . . than to risk coming into conflict with the rigid expectations or the uncompromising, preconceived pattern into which teachers felt all endeavors should fit.

To a person attempting to analyze the situation the greatest need seemed to be (a) to inspire these teachers to a sense of the importance of their service to children and to society and so make teaching more than a job; (b) to release tensions and inhibitions and stimulate creativity through building trust and confidence between the supervisory and administrative staff and the teachers.

There were excellent leadership qualities among the elementary school supervisors concerned with the problem. They were aware of the difficulties and eager to change the attitudes so evident among the teaching staff. They had no doubts about the amount of unreleased ability among the teaching group.

Initial Emphasis Placed on Human Relationships

It was agreed that a warm, human approach to the teacher-supervisor relationship was the first step. It was necessary to give teachers assurance that someone cared and was willing to do something about their problems. Praise and concern for the contribution of all, no matter how meager, had to be the backlog of a program that would draw teachers into their rightful place in the school system.

The supervisory group determined:

—to have friendly, sincere concern for teachers as persons.
—to focus attention on the needs of youngsters in the classroom rather than on the teacher herself and her techniques.
—to overlook many faulty techniques until confidence could be established and constructive help requested.
—to expose teachers to many rich experiences with no requirements or stresses.
—to establish as many situations as possible in which supervisors and teachers might know each other socially.
—to praise and encourage good attitudes and procedures with the hope that with release of strain and fear would come desired participation and sharing.

Probably the first release of talents and abilities came with the realization by teachers that the supervisors wanted most to share in the classroom situations which were giving trouble or in the teaching-learning situation in which the teachers felt they could do the best job. Through this method of approaching problems, old patterns were gradually broken down and new ones were established.

Many small group meetings to which anyone was welcome, but to which no one was required to come, were planned. The privilege of visiting classrooms in other cities was eagerly seized upon by many teachers. These visits helped to build confidence in their own abilities. Classroom supervision ceased to be an inspectional type of supervision, and supervisors worked more with groups on a consultant basis. Planning and discussion with the principals and the supervisors brought about better understanding between these two groups. Principals came to see the importance of good personal relationships and were aided in giving the specific helps requested by teachers, which in itself bred respect and confidence.

Teacher Leaders Emerge as the Environment Changes

Into this picture was injected a sudden growth in the school population which brought with it new teachers, inexperienced and experienced, from all parts of the country, to work side by side with those who had been employed in the city for a long time. Here was an opportunity for able, experienced teachers to share and help those who were teaching for the first time and those who were making an adjustment to a new situation. Here was a chance to see some of the many good things in the local situation through the eyes of those who had recently entered the system. Here was an opportunity for "leavening the loaf" with able teachers who had much to give. There was need for care that the teachers longer in the service who were insecure and diffident were not overshadowed by those who had much to offer and gave of their talents freely. There was need for care that those who were still insecure, and so pulled away from participation and the sharing of ideas, did not convey their feelings to the teachers who had more recently come into the system.

With encouragement and plans worked out by principals and supervisors, teachers began to share and to visit each other at work within their own buildings. In some buildings this was not advisable as the staff had worked together so long that deep-seated feelings of jealousy and fear were present. These teachers were encouraged to go to other buildings to observe and discuss the things they saw. New schools were opened and here the teachers had many mutual problems which they worked out together. A great variety of classroom situations were included in the plan for observations and the discussions which followed, so that many teachers with many ways of doing things had an opportunity to contribute as well as to visit.

Instructional Improvement Calls for Many Contributions

Coupled with this plan for visiting was a plan for participation in curriculum work which would not make it an added burden to the busy teacher. Individuals and groups of teachers were released from classroom responsibilities for a few days or a few weeks to work on curriculum materials. Workshops in which curriculum problems were discussed and materials developed and written were established after schools were closed in the spring. Teachers who attended were paid for their work.

Teacher committees worked on plans for new buildings, on supply lists, on report cards, on policies and suggestions for the administration. Discussions at meetings were centered on child development and upon ways of meeting the needs of children, as well as upon techniques and methods of work. Leadership for these committees was assumed by teachers, principals, or supervisors who had special interest in a particular problem.

Friendly encouragement and praise for work well done were constantly given by word of mouth, by notes of appreciation and commendation, and by comments to other teachers and principals. Morale was lifted by the satisfactions engendered.

Many opportunities for participating in summer programs in neighboring colleges and universities were given to able teachers who were particularly successful in working with children. Newspaper articles, indicating the abilities of these teachers and the recognition which had been afforded them, and notices in school bulletins established the prestige of these teachers and encouraged others to accept summer responsibilities. The expressions of appreciation from the colleges or universities where summer work was done was good for the teachers who participated.

Plans were furthered to help teachers acquire enough confidence to lead discussions, to talk with parent groups, to participate in the give and take of panel discussions. The initial attempts at this type of service were difficult, but with repetition it became easier. The satisfactions so generated were another means of building a feeling of importance and lifting morale.

A number of changes in principalship assignments gave new impetus to lagging professional interest among the principals. Due to the fact that new elementary schools were opened with the increased enrollment, able teachers were given new responsibilities as principals or vice-principals. By this means morale was lifted and ambitions stirred. Principals came in for their share of opportunities to visit within their own system and in other systems. These visits tended to enlarge visions and to give confidence. Principals were stimulated to watch for special abilities among teachers in their own buildings who could contribute to the in-service education of all teachers.

At present, after five or six years of working along the lines suggested, the morale among the elementary school teachers and principals is high. There is evidence of a feeling of belonging and an easy give and take in all staff relationships.

Sensitivity to Individuals Boosts Morale

The most important characteristic of the group leaders was sensitivity to human relationships—among teachers, between principals and teachers, and among teachers, principals, and supervisors. The faith they had in individuals was expressed in all that they did. Supervisors, through encouragement, praise, and recognition given, helped to establish the feeling that the carrying forward of the objectives of a school system was a group responsibility. They gave expression to their sincere belief that the teachers' part in this undertaking was the most important factor in bringing the objectives to fruition. Gradually the feeling of solidarity which was so much needed broke down the tensions and the indifferences in the teaching staff.

Informality, friendliness, and an earnest desire to work with the staff and follow out their suggestions in the most expeditious ways was evident in all the relationships of the supervisors with principals and teachers.

In order to encourage teachers to participate and share responsibilities for promoting a good school program it was essential that no additional burdens be assumed. The declaration of this belief and the keeping of faith by supervisors and administrators in releasing teachers to visit, to work on curriculum materials, and to meet to discuss problems on school time was reassuring to teachers. Many of them received recognition for their contributions which was far reaching. They knew they had abilities and these abilities were needed in their own school system and in other areas. Morale has been lifted and recognition given by capitalizing upon opportunities for wider service in the system as well as in the state.

The group leaders were well trained and knew from their own experiences the difficulties and problems of the classroom teachers. They were constructive in their approaches and accentuated the positive in all their dealings with teachers.

The abilities of the leaders to inspire teachers about the importance of their service to children and to society was an important characteristic. The widened visions and the enthusiasms of the teachers, which resulted from the lifting of classroom teaching into a higher realm than the one in which it was formerly held, did much to bind the group together. Teachers felt united in a common purpose, which they knew to be of great and lasting importance.

Developing a School Program for Pupils with Significant Speech Defects

The superintendent of a city school system called together approximately thirty elementary school principals to formulate a plan for developing a corrective speech program. The meeting was called in a room with reasonably comfortable seating facilities, good lighting, and a blackboard. The superintendent's secretary was present to take a record of the meeting. Two weeks prior to the meeting the superintendent had written a circular letter to each of the principals stating the subject for discussion and requesting that each principal come to the meeting with data concerning the number and ages of pupils in his school who showed evidence of defective speech. The superintendent also asked the principals to think over in advance their suggestions for the organization of a speech correction program.

Planning Proceeds from Survey Findings

After a brief resumé of the reasons for the group discussion, the superintendent asked each principal to report the result of the school survey. The secretary tabulated the numerical data on the blackboard. The superintendent then stated that many of the principals had already approached him in regard to the proper special instruction of pupils with speech handicaps, and that he was taking it for granted that all present desired to do something about it.

In response to the superintendent's request, the principals suggested that the following problems be discussed:

> A more careful survey by a person specially trained to detect and classify speech defects
>
> Arrangements of daily schedule to permit the withdrawal of selected pupils for specific speech therapy during school hours two or three times a week
>
> The provision of appropriate space and facilities for such special supplementary classes
>
> The assignment or employment of teachers specially trained in sufficient number to serve the pupils in need of such instruction according to the schedule planned

The arrangement of transportation between schools of such special teachers

The supervision and administration of the speech correction program.

In order to discuss these specific problems the superintendent, with the advice of the principals, set the date for a second meeting and appointed committees of three persons to formulate recommendations regarding each of the problems indicated above.

At this second meeting the several committees reported, and their reports were discussed and revised by the group as a whole. After the main outline of the plan had been agreed upon, a time was set several months in advance at which the program would commence operation. A committee of two volunteered, at the superintendent's request, to formulate a statement which each principal could use in discussing the matter with his faculty. It was agreed that, after such faculty meetings had been held, any further suggestions or amendments which the teachers presented would be returned to the superintendent; and, if necessary, he would call a third meeting of the principals to discuss minor revisions.

The Leader Facilitates Movement

In this series of meetings, the group leader facilitated a successful outcome by the following characteristics:

> He planned the procedures, the timing, and the situation so that the group members would be comfortable, have sufficient time, and have opportunity for participation.
>
> He made it clear that the group thinking of his principals was essential and would count.
>
> He gave and demanded that the group give courteous attention to each principal's suggestion.
>
> He used light and humorous techniques to keep the group members from straying too far from the matter in hand.
>
> He took time to draw out from the group the essential problems, even though he could have foreseen most of them for himself.
>
> He took his full share in carrying out the recommendations of the group.

Planning a New School Plant

The teacher in the practice of his art makes application of what science has discovered about humans as individuals and as group members. The science of education contributes to individual and common good in proportion to the teacher's insight, knowledge, and skill. However, without adequate facilities and tools, these qualities of the good teacher are heavily discounted and the fine aims of the educational system amount to little. These facts are obvious and are worthy of mention only because educational planning so frequently neglects to consider problems of supply, building design, and finance. Yet these matters determine to a very large extent what the educational program will be.

The Business Manager Is a Group Member

Not often does one find that educational planning conferences include school business officials. Unless they are included in the educational planning it is to be expected that the business manager, for example, may come to think mainly in terms of the budget, of prices, of savings, and may forget the purpose for which the whole school system operates —the best possible education of children. No successful business would ever neglect to keep its purchasing agent informed as to possible changes in the product, or its plant construction and maintenance department advised of needs. They would, in fact, be active participants in all matters which had to do with improving procedure, processes, and the product. One might call this simply good business or he might call it democratic planning. Whatever it is, it is the most efficient way to operate and is too little practiced in school systems.

If this practice were followed it would bring together the contributions of all into a plan which could be expected to succeed through the cooperative efforts of all. The teachers' and supervisors' plans would be geared more realistically to possibilities of practical building design, finance, and supply; and, on the other hand, those whose chief responsibilities are the business activities of the schools would find a new challenge in providing the right tools and facilities in necessary quantity. Out of such democratic process would come a better educational program. Belief in the efficacy of such a process motivated those who planned the Oakland, California, school building program.

Available Funds Condition Planning

In 1945 the citizens of Oakland voted a $15,432,000 bond issue for school building purposes. It was known by the administration of the schools that the money was insufficient to meet all of the school needs. Just how far short it would turn out to be was not fully appreciated by anyone at the time, for there had not been opportunity following the war to correct the estimates of the studies of building needs made prior to the war. Nor could anyone accurately predict how high building costs might go. It soon became evident that the money would meet less than half of Oakland's school housing needs. Population had increased thirty-five percent in five years and, though there had been but a five percent increase in school population during the same five-year period, if all the children under five who lived in Oakland remained there to attend school the school population would increase fifty percent by 1953. Building costs had jumped from about $6.50 per square foot prior to the war to about $13.50.

It was certain that economy in design and equipment of school buildings would be stressed by many, especially by those responsible for financing. Soon many proposals were being made. One suggestion which received quite a bit of support was that as many classrooms should be produced as possible at the expense of auditoriums, gymnasiums, libraries, cafeterias, and other auxiliary facilities. It was insisted upon by some that classrooms should be made as small as possible. According to others, such modern design as acoustic treatment and linoleum floors, which are expensive, should be eliminated. Other persons and groups, without having considered general needs, were certain that facilities should be included for their particular use. In one instance, had these requests been granted, the design of an elementary school would have provided six fully equipped kitchens for the exclusive use of the Parent-Teachers Association, Dads' Club, home teacher, youth groups, and teachers of the school, in addition to the cafeteria kitchen. How could all these various ideas and conflicting opinions be resolved and a practical and educationally sounding building program emerge?

Organization for Planning and Executing Is Completed

The first step was to set up an organization which would insure participation in planning and execution of plans by all who were concerned—teachers, principals, supervisors, business officials, engineers and architects, superintendents, and the Board of Education. Such a plan of organization was proposed to the Board of Education and they approved it readily. The Board took the lead by organizing itself into a Committee of the Whole to meet each Tuesday for consideration of all matters requiring board action in connection with the building program. There was appointed a Building Advisory Committee consisting of teachers, principals, supervisors, superintendents, and members from the Architectural Engineering and Business Departments. This committee was given the responsibility of assisting in developing and approving design standards for all schools and responsibility for approving preliminary and final plans of buildings as well as the task of setting up equipment standards. Committees of teachers to consider special problems such as home economics, science, and industrial arts were authorized by the Board of Education.

It was felt that authorization by the Board would give status to the work of all committees, and such has proved true. Another important aspect of organization was the requirement that all plans of specific buildings be referred to the faculties of such schools for review and suggestion. Thus the framework for democratic procedures was devised and was given official status.

Action Is Based on Study and Discussion

The actual working out of democratic techniques in practice was not so easy. One of the first problems which arose concerned the question, "How many students should a high school library seat at one time?" The librarians said it should seat ten percent of the school. The architects thought the percentage too high. At first the chairman tried to resolve the difference of opinion by vote of the librarians and administrators. The result, though somewhat favorable to the architects, did not settle matters. Finally, the high school committee proposed a study which would involve a representative sampling of all departments whose students are expected to use the library. This actually included teachers from all departments. Interviews and questionnaires were used and results summarized and mathematical analyses made which resulted in modification of the flat ten percent statement of the librarians to require from more than ten percent seating to less than ten percent, depending upon the size of the school. All were pleased with the final result, even the librarians.

The architects and business representatives were fearful that teachers, principals, and supervisors would propose idealistic, even fantastic solutions to building problems. They anticipated suggestions impossible of design or far beyond anything which could be afforded. Much to their surprise, the architects and business representatives frequently found themselves arguing on the side of the case where they had expected the teachers to be, insisting that design must anticipate future needs and improvements in education.

Each committee chairman, at the beginning of the committee's work, had spent time in having the general city needs and the financial picture made clear. Teachers knew on the average what a sink or ten additional square feet of floor space would cost, and they knew also that money spent for these things could not be spent for other items. Thus the teachers, principals, and supervisors were better informed as to costs and building problems; and architectural and business people were better informed as to educational needs.

The findings and studies of committees were reviewed by the Cabinet of Superintendents and were reported to the Board of Education. As a result of this procedure the following policies were adopted by the Board and have served as guides in the conduct of the building program:

- Priority in the order of construction of buildings will be determined on the basis of educational need. Such needs include factors of safety and health.
- A plan for the expenditure of building funds will be established, based on the above principle, and will be adhered to throughout the building program.
- In matters requiring decision as to whether an expenditure is justified or not, educational values will be given more weight than other factors.
- Partial solutions to building and site problems which fail to provide facilities to carry out a standard educational program or which are not a logical part of an ultimate solution will be avoided.

Guided by these principles which were the outgrowth of much thinking by committees of teachers, principals, and supervisors, as well as by the Board itself, the Board has studiously avoided makeshift solutions to problems. Thus, as far as the money available would reach, effort has been made to achieve complete solutions to building problems; and such necessary auxiliary facilities as auditoriums and gymnasiums have been included. Classrooms have been increased in size and improved in design and equipment.

Democratic Planning Pays Off in Value Received

The sharing of planning has been extended to include studies in population and the development of a master plan for Oakland, but that is another story not to be told here. Evidence seems to warrant the conclusion that democratic group planning techniques pay off in dollars and cents in the business side of education.

Democratic procedures at first may seem slow of results. In the beginning there seemed to be too much talk and argument. Voting was found to be a poor way to settle a matter requiring group action, nor was compromise any better. Unless there could be a complete concurrence there was not complete support of the necessary action. Study, research, and analysis of problems was found to be a better way to settle issues. In the matter of design of classrooms, trial was found very effective. Thus, for example, the business department built a model classroom according to the design of the elementary committee and it was tried out in practice. As a result many changes were made. One might conclude that the desire on the part of group members to reach a group decision and the ability to delineate problems clearly in a related setting involving study, research, analysis, and trial of possible solutions leads to an experimental attitude which increases with practice and brings surprisingly favorable results.

Coordinating Staff Services

Large school systems face a problem of establishing and maintaining lines of communication which will promote democratic group action. As the numbers of schools increase, so do the adminstrative and supervisory services designed to assist the teachers in their endeavor. The flow of information, ideas, and suggestions; the working together in small groups, which are comparatively easy of attainment in small school systems, here become more difficult. The very pressure of numbers increases the need for cooperative group action and, at the same time, poses certain problems in the realization of this goal.

Specialized Supervisory Services Intensify Need for Cooperation

The specialization of supervisory services, which provides excellent assistance to teachers in various fields, in itself intensifies the need for close cooperation among the members of the supervisory staff. Particularly is this true in elementary schools where the teacher is responsible for instruction in all fields. Each teacher usually comes in contact with a general supervisor, a supervisor of music, of art, of physical education, of audio-visual education, of library service, and perhaps others. No matter how democratic and satisfying her relationship with each supervisor may be, the teacher cannot but be confused if she finds differences of philosophy and practice among her several supervisors. At best, she may conclude that the curriculum she plans for her pupils should be more or less compartmentalized, rather than the integrative experiences about which she reads in her courses of study. The close working together of the supervisory staff is essential to a well-rounded program of instruction.

The supervisors of one such city have attempted in various ways to coordinate their services to elementary teachers. At first, two or more supervisors organized meetings to discuss children's experiences in art as they relate to experiences in the social studies, or to present simple dramatic productions in which language arts, music, art, and rhythmic expression were involved. Teachers were interested in trying the new ideas gained from such meetings. An excellent beginning had been made.

A Specific Problem Becomes a Group Concern

The approach of California's centennial focused attention on the history of the state, and at the same time demanded that some guidance be given teachers in planning experiences suitable for children of elementary school age. The supervisory staff, after discussing the matter, decided that they might pool their efforts in assisting teachers of the fourth grade, who commonly carried on studies of the state, find ways of enriching their teaching of early days in California. They would arrange a series of meetings, with attendance voluntary, for this purpose.

Planning the meetings gave the supervisors opportunities to become more familiar with the ways of living in California before 1849, to discover local points of interest hitherto unsuspected, and to locate fresh materials which would be valuable to both teachers and children. The supervisor of libraries, who had made an intensive study of the history of the local area, was of inestimable assistance. It was agreed that the general supervisors would make available reference materials, stories which would stimulate dramatic play, and suggestions for carrying on the study in terms of children's interests and drives to learning. The supervisors of audio-visual education, of art, physical education, and music would suggest ways of enriching the study.

The fourth-grade teachers were eager to help in this field. Large numbers of them attended the meetings regularly and expressed appreciation of the stimulation they received. Classrooms reflected the increased interest, and children found satisfaction in many types of activities that helped them relive the days of the Indians, the Spanish, and the earliest Americans.

Teachers began to take part in the meetings. One teacher whose children had had an unusually rich experience selected favorite bits of their dramatic play to show the entire group. So many interesting and ingenious materials were developed in many classrooms that it was decided to hold an exhibit at the end of the term for the further sharing of ideas. Contributions were numerous and varied: collections made by individual children, candles and adobe bricks made in authentic fashion, models of Indian and Spanish dwellings, dressed dolls, crude costumes and utensils used in dramatic play, small paintings and large murals, simple maps and pictorial time lines, bits of creative writing. Each article represented some experience that had made the study live for children.

This cooperative venture on the part of supervisors and teachers has been effective in many ways. The supervisors have enjoyed the opportunity to work together on a subject broad enough to engage the interest of every one. Their unity of effort has helped teachers see the interrelatedness of all learnings. Their offering of assistance on a voluntary basis has created good feeling toward all members of the staff and has opened the way for further work together. The teachers, who have shared ideas with one another and gained new insight into the learning process, pronounced this series of meetings one of the most helpful they had known. Similar series will be planned with other groups of teachers as time goes on.

Building Community Unity

A four-room school in a small rural area suffered from many serious disciplinary problems. The children were antagonistic toward each other and toward the staff. Low school achievement, irregular attendance, and more serious delinquent acts were common.

As the supervisors and teachers hunted for causes they began to look beyond the school and soon realized that they could find counterparts of the classroom tensions within the community. The "Old-Timers'" Community Club and the "New-Comers'" Parents' Club were set in opposite camps. Each had about fifty members. The older residents resented the new arrivals who were coming in such numbers as to threaten their leadership.

Parents Are Asked To Consider the School's Job

The problem for the teachers was how to breach this gap between the two community groups. They decided to attack the problem indirectly by inviting the parents in to consider how best to meet the needs of the children in a school program. They asked parents to meet in an afternoon session to consider "understanding and helping our children."

The attendance was large. Each group had come prepared to show how the other faction was working against the welfare of the children. Fortunately, the teachers had thought through the program ahead of time and were ready to give the meeting intelligent direction in its early stages. They outlined recent findings on child growth and development and followed a point of view that made bickering about local issues seem ridiculous. The parents quickly caught the spirit of looking for the best for their children. They saw that the insecurity engendered by community differences was developing serious problems in the children and they gave thought to ways of creating the best home, school, and community environment.

Two Groups Become One

It was decided to give dinners at the school to which all members of the community would be invited. Responsibility for preparation and serving the meal was shared by both new and long-time residents. They found many things in common as they worked together. Dances were held and motion pictures shown.

Teachers and parents brought magazine articles to the meetings dealing with the latest teaching practices. Soon the community recognized it had a share in curriculum building. Excursions were taken and classes were invited out to farms to observe latest agricultural methods. Soon the well-established residents, who had most to show in this connection, had drastically changed their attitudes toward both the school and the newcomers. They began to think how best they might help in absorbing the new arrivals into the economic life of the community.

Over one hundred and fifty community members of both factions were included in the group practices in the school. The effectiveness and harmony with which they worked together was clear evidence of the new attitudes.

The change in the school was even more striking. The new community attitude had a profound effect on the students. Cooperation replaced antagonism as the accepted social pattern. At this stage the supervisors again provided an effective service. They had acted as counselors to the teachers from the beginning of the project. While the tense situation still prevailed, they took sociometric measurements of the students and graphically portrayed the strained conditions. Following the change they again took measurements and the new graphs showed major improvements. The combination of teacher evaluations and sociometric charts made evident to both teachers and laymen the greatly improved conditions in the school which had resulted from community cooperation.

Utilizing the Services of Experts

Facing each other in a semicircle in the library of a small town school, sit about forty teachers, principals, with some supervisors, researchers, librarians, counselors, and a consultant. At the side of the room on a table are trays of new books for reference reading in language arts, child development, evaluation, and general education. Against the front wall is a blackboard covered with a pattern of general education for teenagers which the consultant has just presented. The group is questioning the consultant in general education in an easy give-and-take manner. This atmosphere prevails because he has worked before with the staff of this rural-urban county and understands their problems. The county coordinator and several others are taking notes so that the highlights of this meeting may be distributed at the next meeting. To these records will be added a bibliography on intergroup relations, an inventory on reading interests, three evaluation forms which teachers have made with their classes, and an excerpt from a book on the developmental tasks of adolescents. At the same time, county staff members are observing the responses of participants in order to make informal comment on the progress of the group in the next planning session. At the end of this first meeting each member of the group writes "Ideas or Problems Which I Suggest that the Consultant Discuss."

The County Office Takes the Lead

This conference was the first of a series of twelve during which teachers from the seventh through the twelfth grades, together with five expert consultants and county staff members, studied some problems of language arts in general education. The plan of the series was incorporated in a letter from the county department of instruction to the administrators in which the plan and procedure were set forth. An excerpt from that letter follows:

> While the conferences stem from a need to develop a flexible county language arts program from kindergarten through the twelfth grade, they will be *limited to teachers, problems, and techniques in grades seven through twelve*. However, attention will be directed to the elementary foundations.
>
> To make results of the conferences really effective in the schools, principals with their staffs should decide about becoming participating schools. Wherever possible, a nucleus of two or more delegates should represent each school. Those who register are expected to attend all twelve meetings.
>
> The Principals' Advisory Committee for Language Arts has included in the plan the recommendation that completion of the twelve conferences be considered the equivalent of two units of work in satisfying one of the possible "hurdles" in the salary scale. The entire county-sponsored service is without cost to teachers.
>
> To summarize, this county staff service, planned with the Principals' Advisory Committee and the five consultants in the state college, is to help the
>
> —individual teachers to develop interests and skills
> —schools to improve their programs in language arts
> —county to develop a guide for language arts
>
> The conferences will be
> —practical and specific
> —with instructional materials available
> —well coordinated with a weekly summary of the conference distributed between meetings.

The Varied Participant Roles Are Defined

Several of the meetings utilized different methods to induce group development, participation, and production. For example, in the third conference, the time was divided between the presentation of the consultant and discussions in seven small groups led by county staff members. The county supervisors were in the role of stimulators of participation. They did not act as specialists in language arts but as advocates for the development of children. The consultant, the staff psychologist, and the coordinator had the role of resource people in as many groups as they found time to join. They contributed ideas as they seemed to be needed. In order to operate effectively, the supervisor-leaders together with the consultant agreed upon the following duties. These were mimeographed together with a time schedule and distributed at the beginning of the meeting.

The consultant with the coordinator and the county psychologist will visit as many groups as time will permit. Use them as sources of reference.

The leader-supervisors of each of the seven groups will encourage people to become acquainted and feel free to express their ideas.
—Refer questions to members rather than give answers or do all the talking.
—Include the consultant as a participant or as resource expert.
—Wait while participants use seconds of silence for reflective thinking rather than press responses.
—Insure that all expressed feelings of the members are understood adequately by the group.
—Reflect the attitudes and opinions of the group rather than those of the leader.
—Take time to summarize the groups' feelings and contributions.
—Close the meeting graciously but firmly at 5:45 P. M.

The members will have opportunity to exchange ideas and gain understandings. Talk with each other. Speak freely as a recognized member of the group. Give reactions to the first three meetings.
—What is valuable in the consultant's presentation?
—What does not make sense?
—What are special problems in my school?
—How can the ideas presented be put to work in my class?

The recorder will keep a detailed account of the meeting.
—Write the questions raised by members.
—Record the highlights of the discussion.
—Summarize at appropriate intervals.
—Give the notes to the leader at the end of the meeting.

The observers are the county staff members who will report to the next planning session.
—Study the behavior of participants.
—Note whether responses and actions promote interaction and the progress of group thinking.

The general chairman is the coordinator who, with the associate for this meeting, the county staff psychologist, will edit the record of the presentation of the consultant and those of the seven conference groups.

Problems for Consideration Are Many and Real

As the twelve conferences progressed through the weeks, the consultant-experts and participants explored problems, experiences, and skills pertinent to language arts. By various procedures they delved into general education for all youth: language arts in general education; the maturing of teen-agers; evaluation of outcomes in language arts in terms of behavior; communication through writing, speaking, and listening; communication through reading; guidance functions of teaching in language arts; evaluation instruments in language arts; language arts from kindergarten through the sixth grade; commitment of each of the participating schools to its next step.

In order to plan the next step, a census of "What Is Your Opinion?" was made at the eighth meeting by means of a questionnaire. Other outcomes in addition to those collected in "What Is Your Opinion?" were evident not only in study group meetings cropping up in schools but also in reports of teachers.

One remarked, "I tried an inventory of reading. It gave me some ideas in a short time."

A principal asked, "Our teachers want to talk with the high school teachers about the articulation problem. Will you meet with us, too?"

The advisory council and supervisors said to the coordinator, "Let's get together on the county guide."

The Consultant Renders a Distinct Service

In studying the movement to gauge any rapid progress, slow motion, or backsliding, the county staff was aware of the invaluable contributions of a service team of consultants judiciously chosen. The five experts contributed not only from their special studies but planned and acted as an organic unit participating with professional design and color as well as substance. Not only did the county staff and consultants plan as a group, but the second consultant on the schedule attended the two meetings of the first one in order to brief himself.

These well-selected consultants saved the group an enormous amount of time because they skimmed the wealth of resources at their command in light of the professional maturing of group members. When teachers desire to improve their work, they do not want to raise themselves by their own bootstraps. They wish to begin thinking together at the place where they are and with the best resources of personnel and materials available. Nothing wears out teachers more than committees which ineptly begin at the beginning of philosophy and practice as though no one had ever worked through similar problems. In contrast, of course, is the group led by those who accept anything and everything willy-nilly to avoid the irksome duty of thinking for themselves and with others.

Some unique functions executed by the five experts indicate their assistance in promoting a long-range program. First of all, they aided the group to work through its own problems. In order to do this, they:

—created an atmosphere that is permissive and comfortable and with some regard for group metabolism.
—built rapport between experts and group members as well as between members. They liked to be together and they anticipated the next meeting.
—presented materials well organized through various appropriate methods . . . in contrast to rambling through some of their disjointed experiences.
—offerings were tailor-made to fit the stature and color of the individuals in the group.
—drew on the county schools for illustrations as a source of meaningful material. They utilized the professional experiences of the participants.
—allowed sufficient time for group thinking so that the participants did not have to hurdle too many steps at once.
—planned the scope of problems within feasible limits of time and effort to raise the sights on educational problems.
—helped leaders to emerge to work with subcommittees and follow-up studies.
—practiced the techniques of acceptable group procedures by becoming listeners, tellers, questioners, or silent partners as their leadership and expertness merged with the best interests of the group.
—gave a perspecive to the unexpected remarks or actions which offered clues. This indicated a professional and social maturity most desirable in experts.
—helped the members of the group to change. The teachers advanced to a firmer basis of understanding maturing teen-age boys and girls and how communication through language arts may improve their general education.

When does a supervisor include the services of experts? When the group needs more power to operate more effectively.

Studying the Community

"You have two years free from supervision duties. Devote them to the development of school-community teamwork throughout the county." With these instructions one supervisor in a small rural county found himself engaged on an interesting project, made financially possible by a grant from the Rosenberg Foundation of San Francisco.

Common Problems Make for Group Feeling

There can be a team only where a number of persons recognize a common problem. While the county superintendent of schools in this county and a small number of community leaders could agree that there were many serious problems facing both school and community, there was no commonly held opinion on the subject; and, consequently, there was no rallying point about which to develop teamwork. In view of this, the supervisor felt that the logical starting point would be a community self-analysis.

There were other reasons for making such a start. The actual facts gathered would be of the greatest value not only in indicating problems on which to work, but also in showing how to go about solving them. By including a large number of people in the survey there would be a large number prepared to go into the action stage to meet the problems.

The first step was to suggest to the chairman of the Recreation Commission for the county seat, a city of three thousand, that he call together a small group of school and community leaders who saw most clearly the needs of the community. This small committee agreed that it would be sound strategy to survey the county seat and its immediate surrounding area and later to encourage other county centers to make a similar study. It was felt that to study the county as a unit would be impractical in view of the complication of having many meetings with people over a large area.

This committee then drew up a list of the forty most active community and school leaders and invited them to a meeting. The supervisor personally gave the invitations and explained the possibilities of the project to each. All came, an almost unheard-of event in this highly organized and busy town.

The meeting gave enthusiastic support to the project and worked out the general procedure. The life of the community was divided into eleven areas: adult education, community economics, crime and delinquency, curriculum, government, health, home life, minority groups, recreation, religion, and welfare.

Agreement on Procedures Is Reached

The group selected a chairman for each area and gave him instructions to complete his committee in consultation with the supervisor and a small steering committee. Agreement was reached on the following procedure and plans:

1. The committees were to devote their first meeting to a general review of their subject and to consider the kind of information they would require for adequate planning. This meeting would clear the air of vigorously held points of view and prepare the committee members to work with each other. The next two or three meetings—whatever proved to be necessary—would be devoted to listing questions and general information required for planning. Some of the information would be quickly obtained from documents. Generally, it would involve questioning teachers, parents, community leaders, businessmen, and students

2. The questions from all of the committees were then to be grouped under appropriate persons to be questioned. For example, the questionnaire to teachers might include questions from several committees.

3. Each committee member would be asked to assist in administering the questionnaires to one of the groups.

4. The answers would be summarized and the information returned to the committee requesting it.

5. The committees would consider the facts and make recommendations for action based on this information.

6. When the findings and recommendations were all in, they would be duplicated and assembled in loose-leaf form. These reports would then be circulated among community leaders and educators. Community forums and talks before various service groups would also be used to make the community sensitive to its problems and the steps needed to remedy them.

Original Plans Must Be Modified

The original plan was followed, with a few exceptions. It was thought that the early meetings would deal chiefly with listing the questions that should be answered in order to get the facts on which to plan. However, many members came with fixed ideas and had recommendations to make the first day. These recommendations were accepted as hypotheses, and the question of discovering whether the facts would justify them arose. This less formal approach added vigor to meetings and the results were good.

Another deviation came when the Chamber of Commerce took over the "Community Economics Committee" as a subcommittee of that organization. This had real advantages. Problems such as housing and the encouragement of new business, which were beyond the scope of the committee, could be turned over when they arose to the appropriate Chamber of Commerce committees for consideration. There are, however, serious limitations to having one organization take over a committee. It means that only one segment of the total community is represented.

In larger, more highly stratified urban areas, this factor would be even more important.

Another variation occurred in the presentation of findings. The Recreation Committee presented its findings to the total community well before the rest of the committees were finished because of special circumstances calling for immediate action. Such flexibility is an advantage. In a similar manner the Committee on Economics came out well ahead of the others. While this meant distributing questionnaires before all committees were ready to contribute to them, it was possible to include questions from several committees and only a minimum of resurveying was necessary.

The supervisor's job was a busy one. He acted as secretary for the various committees; planned all meetings carefully with the respective chairmen; discussed questions with the committee members, who frequently came to the supervisor's office; reported to community clubs on the progress of committees; and kept the schools informed of the findings. The panel technique became a popular way of working with these groups and agencies.

The Recreation Committee Shares Questionnaire Findings

Since the Recreation Committee reached the stage of decision first, its organization and work are described in detail. Its work is typical of that of the other committees since they all followed a somewhat similar plan. The variance in the points of view held in the community are revealed by the following quotations:

> "It will be a crime if you add to the recreational opportunities of our young people. Already my two children are out most nights. They never have time to do their homework. What good will come of adding another out-of-home distraction?"

> "If the community does not get busy and provide some sort of a youth center, it will be a crime. These kids hang around the pool halls and the street corners half of the night looking for trouble. They are just healthy, vigorous kids. Why can't the community and school get together and provide some decent recreational opportunities?"

These statements served as a starting point for the work of the Recreation Committee. Headed by the Methodist minister, a highly respected leader with extensive experience in youth work, the committee included the president of the Women's Club, the chairman and secretary of the Recreation Commission, the physical education teachers of the secondary and elementary schools, a local scoutmaster, and the school supervisor who acted as secretary. As the members examined their own experiences with youngsters, they found the same conflict as that described in the two quotations. To get at the facts, it was decided to draft questionnaires for students, parents, teachers, and community leaders. These questionnaires were to obtain a picture of present conditions in recreation and to get an indication of felt needs. While the committee members, working in pairs, drafted the items, the chairman and secretary made a brief survey of the commercial recreational opportunities in the city.

From the data gathered from the questionnaire to the students and the survey of commercial activities, the committee reached the following conclusions. These, together with the facts that substantiated them, they submitted to the community at a large public meeting.

There is a real need for increased recreational opportunity for youth.

The recreational program should be county-wide.

There should be a full-time director.

Municipal governments should provide local facilities; the county government should provide the director.

The county program should be closely integrated with the present local programs.

The county program and local programs should be closely integrated with the schools' program.

Any program involving youth should be led by youth.

Youth Shares in Planning

Before the time of the public meeting at which the findings and recommendations were presented, the young people held a special meeting with the supervisor and decided that since they were going to speak on the leadership role of youth they would do something about its implementation at the same time. They prepared a plan whereby they would have a youth delegation go to the five high schools of the county and present the recreational program to the student bodies for approval and suggestions. Each would be asked to appoint three members to a county youth committee that would be empowered to establish a recreational program with an adult group acting as advisers.

The community meeting was highly successful. The supervisor outlined the findings of the student questionnaire. Each of the seven principles was explained and defended by a member of the committee; and all seven were enthusiastically endorsed. The plan proposed by the youth group was also adopted and an adult committee was appointed to back this group in every way possible.

The youth group was expanded to include both high school students and alumni to twenty-four years of age. While it was decided to work through the high schools in the initial stages of organizing, all committees were to include alumni and other young people in the same age group.

The questionnaire to the students had provided so much data that the committee decided not to make such a complete survey of the other community groups. The questionnaire to parents was administered to a small group through the PTA and returns tended to validate those of the questionnaire to students. The feeling of a large group of community leaders was obtained at a public meeting of the Recreation Commission. The reactions of the teachers were obtained at a staff meeting. All groups supported the idea that there was a real recreational need and that concerted action on a county-wide basis was the best approach.

While group questioning has many disadvantages, it was felt that the answer from the questionnaire to the students had been so definite that the great additional amount of work that would be involved in individually administering the questionnaire to all community leaders, teachers, and parents was not justified. The questionnaires would have had to be administered at a time when the adults in the community were very busy with other activities, and the task would have been particularly difficult. The committee members were converts to the principle of keeping fact finding as simple as possible.

Leadership Constantly Changes

The survey committee, having studied the situation and made recommendations, felt that its task was completed. Leadership for carrying out the recommendations was passed to the youth committee and the adult consultant group. Actually, many of the personnel who were on the survey committee are also involved in the next steps. The supervisor, as a status leader, acts as a counselor for the student group as they visit the county schools and organize their County Youth Committee.

The group processes carried on by the Recreation Committee and the other area survey committees show promise of rich returns. Even before they have been completed there is considerable concrete evidence of an improved level of living in both school and community. Should the concept and techniques of cooperative planning by all members of the community become established, the possibilities of community improvement are limitless.

The Role of the Supervisor in Utilizing Group Processes

What were the characteristics of leadership exhibited by the supervisors which made group processes in these situations so successful? What functions did the supervisors serve? As one examines the role played by the supervisors in the situations described, the following behaviors are evident:

1. They helped the groups to define their goals and delineate their problems.
2. They established a cooperative, permissive atmosphere which freed the participants so that they contributed their best thinking to the solution of the group's problems.
3. They utilized the various talents and knowledge of the members of the group in arriving at decisions.
4. They had a genuine regard and appreciation for the worth of each individual and a willingness to understand and accept each one at his own level of growth.
5. They enlisted the help of outside resources; they did not give answers, but helped to provide experiences through which teachers and lay groups found their own answers.
6. They planned the procedures, the timing, and the situation so that the group members would be comfortable, have sufficient time, and have opportunity to participate.
7. They allowed sufficient time for group thinking so that the participants did not have too many hurdles to make at one time.
8. They practiced the technique of acceptable group procedures by becoming listeners, tellers, questioners, and silent partners as their leadership and expertness merged with the best interests of the group.
9. They coordinated effort, helped the members of the group to change, and moved the group to action.
10. They instilled in others the desire to belong, to participate, and to take responsibility for and pride in the work of the group.
11. They discovered skills, competencies, interests, and abilities so that each, while taking part in group processes, gained the maximum security which results from having a part to play and a contribution to make.
12. They relinquished leadership to other members of their groups but continued to serve as consultants and advisers, to clear obstacles, and revive flagging enthusiasm.
13. They provided materials and resources and made available research studies and data to aid the groups in their work.
14. They evaluated themselves continually to see that their purposes were valid; that good human relationships were observed; that the steps in group processes were followed; that they were not moving too fast for their group; and that the work of the groups was in keeping with the over-all program of the schools.
15. They were, above all, sensitive to group techniques and to human relationships among teachers, between teachers and principals, and among teachers, principals, and supervisors.

Selected Bibliography

(In addition to references cited in Chapter II)

American Council on Education. *Sociometric Work Guide for Teachers.* Washington, D. C.: American Council on Education, 1947. 90 p. (mimeographed).

Barnes, Fred. "A College Class Discovers Group Dynamics," *Educational Leadership,* V (February 1948). p. 306-12.

Bavelas, Alex, and Lewin, Kurt. "Training in Democratic Leadership," *Journal of Abnormal and Social Psychology,* XXXVII (January 1942). p. 115-19.

Benne, Kenneth. *A Conception of Authority.* Teachers College Contribution to Education No. 895. New York: Bureau of Publications, Teachers College, 1945.

Benne, Kenneth; Bradford, Leland; and Lippitt, Ronald. "Toward Improved Skill in Group Living: A Discussion," *Educational Leadership,* V (February 1948). p. 286-94.

Bradford, Leland, and Lippitt, Ronald. "Building a Democratic Work Group," *Personnel,* XXII (November 1945).

Bradford, Leland, and Lippitt, Ronald. "Role-Playing in Supervisory Training," *Personnel,* Volume 22, No. 6, 1946.

Cantor, Nathaniel. *The Dynamics of Learning.* Buffalo, New York: Foster and Stewart Publishing Company, 1946.

Coyle, Grace L. *Studies in Group Behavior.* New York: Harper and Brothers, 1937. 258 p.

Cunningham, Ruth. "Getting the Group Habit," *Educational Leadership,* IV (March 1947). p. 380-85.

Cushman, C. Leslie, and Prall, Charles E. *Teacher Education in Service.* Washington, D. C.: American Council on Education, 1944. 503 p.

Elliott, Harrison S. *The Process of Group Thinking.* New York: Association Press, 1928. 229 p.

Follett, Mary P. *Dynamic Administration.* New York: Harper and Brothers, 1942. 320 p.

Giles, H. H. *Teacher-Pupil Planning.* New York: Harper and Brothers, 1941.

Goslin, Willard E. "When We Work Together," *Educational Leadership,* I (January 1944). p. 221-25.

Graham, Jessie. "A Workshop for Supervisors," *Educational Leadership,* V (February 1948). p. 333-36.

Judson, L. S., and Judson, Ellen. *Modern Group Discussion: Public and Private.* New York: H. W. Wilson Company, 1937.

Koopman, George R.; Miel, Alice; and Misner, Paul J. *Democracy in School Administration.* New York: D. Appleton Century Company, 1943. 330 p.

Lewin, Kurt. "Field Theory of Learning," Nelson, H. B., (Editor), *The Psychology of Learning, Forty-First Yearbook* of the National Society for the Study of Education, Part II. Bloomington, Illinois: Public School Publishing Company, 1942.

―――――. "Group Decision and Social Change," Newcomb, Theodore, and Hartley, Eugene, (Editors), in *Readings in Social Psychology*. New York: Henry Holt and Company, 1947. p. 330-44.

Lieberman, Joshua (Editor). *New Trends in Group Work*. New York: Association Press, 1938. 229 p.

Lippitt, Ronald, and White, R. K. "An Experimental Study of Leadership and Group Life," Newcomb, Theodore, and Hartley, Eugene (Editors), *Readings in Social Psychology*. New York: Henry Holt and Company, 1947. p. 315-30.

Lippitt, Ronald. "The Morale of Youth Groups," Watson, G. (Editor), *Civilian Morale*. New York: Houghton Mifflin Company, 1942. Chapter VII.

Lippitt, Ronald; Hendry, Charles; and Zander, Alvin. "Reality Practice as an Educational Method," *Sociometry*, Volume 7, No. 2, 1944.

Lippitt, Ronald; Bradford, Leland; and Benne, Kenneth. "Sociodramatic Clarification of Leader and Group Roles," *Sociatry*, I (March 1947). p. 82-91.

Miel, Alice. "Let's Work Together on the Curriculum," *Educational Leadership*, V (February 1948), p. 294-300.

―――――, "A Group Studies Itself to Improve Itself," *Teachers College Record*, XLIX (October 1947). p. 31-43.

Moreno, Jacob L., and Jennings, H. H. "Sociometric Methods of Grouping and Re-Grouping," *Sociometry*, VII (November 1944). p. 397-414.

Moreno, Jacob L. *Who Shall Survive?* New York: Beacon House Publishing Company, 1948. 435 p.

National Education Association, Department of Supervision and Directors of Curriculum. *Cooperation: Principles and Practices*, Eleventh Yearbook. Washington, D. C.: The Department, 1938. 244 p.

Slavson, Samuel L. *Creative Group Education*. New York: Association Press, 1945. 247 p.

Smith, Othaniel, and Dolio, A. J. "Recent Developments in Grouping— A Minimum Bibliography," *Educational Leadership*, IV (March 1947). p. 403-11.

―――――. "A Supplement to a Minimum Bibliography in Grouping," *Educational Leadership*, V (February 1948). p. 337.